Chowgirls

Killer Party Food

Chowgirls

Killer Party Food

....

RIGHTEOUS BITES & COCKTAILS
FOR EVERY SEASON

HEIDI ANDERMACK & AMY LYNN BROWN

ARSENAL
PULP PRESS
VANCOUVER

ARSENAL PULP PRESS
Suite 202 – 211 East Georgia St.
Vancouver, BC V6A 1Z6
Canada
arsenalpulp.com

The authors and publisher assert that the information contained in this book is true and complete to the best of their knowledge. All recommendations are made without the guarantee on the part of the author and publisher. The authors and publisher disclaim any liability in connection with the use of this information. For more information, contact the publisher.

Note for our UK readers: measurements for non-liquids are for volume, not weight.

Cover design by Robert Pflaum
Interior food photographs by Jennifer Marx
Cover photograph by Shelly Mosman
Author photograph by Sarah Whiting

Edited by Susan Safyan

Typeset in Adrianna, GFY Woodward, and Dickens McQueen fonts by Chank.com

Printed and bound in Canada

Library and Archives Canada Cataloguing in Publication:

Brown, Amy, 1969-, author
        Chowgirls killer party food : righteous bites & cocktails for every
season / Amy Lynn Brown & Heidi Andermack.

CONTENTS

PREFACE

We couldn't be happier to bring you this, our first cookbook and the culmination of a lifelong dream, *Chowgirls Killer Party Food*. We hope this collection of bite-sized delights and small, handcrafted recipes will make its way into your home kitchen and become a go-to resource for your party planning. Many of the recipes in this book have been on our catering menu for more than ten years; they're proven winners that have guests chasing down our service staff for more.

Because we're located in the American Midwest, we enjoy distinct seasons that influence our choice of ingredients. We've categorized our recipes into seasons so you can easily shop for ingredients perfect for spring, summer, fall, or winter gatherings. (No matter where you live, most ingredients are readily available.)

The Twin Cities of Minneapolis and St. Paul are well known for robust farmers' market and food co-op scenes, forerunners in the national trend for organics. As such, we were early adopters of sustainable cooking, the first catering company of our kind here in Minnesota. Our hope is that you'll source ingredients close to home, allowing your region's local purveyors to help your food shine!

Perhaps most importantly, we started Chowgirls with a shared passion for expressing ourselves creatively through cooking. Feel free to personalize and adapt our offerings to make them your own.
Be inspired, share, enjoy!

—HEIDI ANDERMACK & AMY LYNN BROWN

INTRODUCTION

RECIPES

We've chosen recipes that work best for celebrations of eight to twenty guests. A large portion of our business is dedicated to creating parties, weddings, and corporate events for 300 people or more, so most of the recipes can be scaled up to larger quantities if needed.

The cocktail formulas create batch drinks for eight to twelve guests and also can be doubled or tripled, making it easy to serve sophisticated and impressive "craft" cocktails without the need for a hipster bartender at your party. We also include tips for garnishes and glassware that should enhance your ability to look like a pro.

RESOURCEFULNESS

Off-premises caterers like ourselves spend a lot of time working in challenging environments—like artist warehouses, where our only access to running water is a janitor's sink. We once rocked a wedding in the Boundary Waters Canoe Area, a nationally protected wilderness area in Minnesota's Superior National Forest, where we had to transport all our equipment and food in by canoe, then hike it all the way into a primitive campsite for preparation. At another wilderness wedding, this one in Wisconsin, we had to cook a meal for 100 over a wood fire and use water from a lake to rinse 350 dinner plates. Through these experiences, we've learned how to make amazing dishes under any circumstances.

A big part of our success is being able to prepare not simultaneously finished dishes but rather components of dishes that are pulled together just before serving. We encourage you to work in a similar way. Make sauces, dressings, and spreads a day or two ahead of your party, then focus on the finished product right before serving. Simply "thinking like a caterer" can increase your chances of smooth party-throwing tenfold.

CULTURE

Beyond the logistics of catering, our business decisions are driven by our values. Despite an already large and ever-growing list of staffers, we prioritize a culture of kindness and humanity. Even as the company grows more corporate in terms of its size, we recognize that we're real people, and that's reflected in our food and service. This casual approach has helped us to retain smart, fun, and talented staff. Chowgirls' on-site servers don't wear bowties or pantyhose—heck, we didn't even get our first uniforms until our business was ten years old! But our service is respectful and professional, helpful and personal. Everyone is casual, genuine, warm, and funny, just like you, dear reader!

We've all been trained to keep our cool, even in the most stressful of catering emergencies. You're running behind, you've burned your crostini, and now there are ten extra guests who didn't RSVP? Never let on that anything's awry; let the guests enjoy your party without revealing those worries, and you'll all be more relaxed in the long run. A favorite mantra of ours is, "It's just food, not a medical emergency." If you've got the right people at your party, you'll all figure out a way to have fun, even if the canapés come out thirty minutes late.

SUSTAINABILITY

Just four years after launching Chowgirls, we received our first-ever award from **Minnesota Bride** magazine. Until then, the category of "Best Green Caterer" didn't exist; the editor created it especially for us because she was so impressed with our commitment to the environment and the community. Since then, we've been featured in dozens of articles about how to do things right and are often consulted about how to grow a food-based company that puts its money where its mouth is when it comes to sustainability.

Over the years, we've created guidelines to help ourselves and our staff understand what we do and why we do it. We're sharing that information with you here, not just to give you a better idea of who we are, but to give you ideas on how to make food choices that are good for you and your guests.

CHOWGIRLS FOOD VALUES

We choose our ingredients first and foremost on the basis of being seasonal and local, organic, and Fair Trade. Here's why:

SEASONAL & LOCAL

We've organized this cookbook seasonally, starting with spring and ending with winter, because we strive to prepare food that's appropriate for each season, both in terms of flavor and ingredient availability. This supports Mother Nature's cycles rather than the all-too-common attitude that we should be able to get whatever we want, whenever and wherever we want it.

Seasonal food also has better flavor and quality. In our part of North America, a strawberry in June is exciting, full of sweetness and color. A December strawberry shipped in from Mexico, unripe and bland, is not much more than a commodity, a colorful thing to put on a plate. Asparagus is available in our region only for a short time each year, making it a special treat to savor during the early spring. At Chowgirls, we feature asparagus items from mid-April through June. Zucchini is part of our vegetable platter in the summer and early fall, but not in January (Isn't everybody sick of zucchini by October, anyhow?). Fresh berries aren't used past October. During the winter months, we try to use only dried fruits and nuts for garnish and cold-storage vegetables like beets, butternut squash, sunchokes, and Brussels sprouts for entrées and side dishes.

Part of the beauty of using seasonally available produce is that it's easier to source ingredients that are local, bridging the gap between farmers, grocery stores, food co-ops, and you, the cook. When food is imported from another climate on the other side of the globe, environmental resources are expended, the local economy is not supported, and, at the end of it all, flavor is compromised, as the food is kept in cold storage for extended periods of time. Furthermore, purchasing local food is a way to know our farmers and food sources and encourage a strong economy in our neighborhoods, cities, and region.

Our first choice is always local or regionally grown and produced ingredients. When needed items aren't available locally, our second choice is for them to be grown elsewhere in the US or Canada. The last resort is foods from outside of North America, such as bananas, coffee, and chocolate, which must be imported. Our best options for items like these are to buy them organic and Fair Trade.

ORGANIC & NON-GMO

It's well known that organic food, grown without the use of pesticides, is significantly less harmful to humans, animals, and the environment than conventionally grown fare. Sometimes we opt for local food that isn't "certified" organic but is grown with organic standards and fair-labor practices. Certain types of produce, such as berries and potatoes, are more subject to pesticide contamination, so we always source them organically. Other foods, like citrus fruits, are less affected by conventional growing techniques, and we're more likely to substitute the non-organic version than skip them altogether. We rely on the Environmental Working Group's (EWG) Dirty Dozen and Clean Fifteen, each a Shopper's Guide to Pesticides in Produce. To get EWG's most up-to-date guides, visit their website at ewg.org.

We also prefer non-genetically modified (GM) ingredients. Most processed food typically contains one or more ingredients derived from genetically engineered crops. Because US law doesn't require the labeling of genetically engineered produce, if you want to avoid GM crops, purchase organically grown foods or items bearing the "Non-GMO Project Verified" seal.

FAIR TRADE

Chowgirls believes in building community and supporting individuals who share our values. Oftentimes, in big agriculture, workers' quality of life may be compromised (poor work conditions, low pay, unhealthy environment) and even endangered (enslavement, dangerous work conditions). We prefer to use ingredients from companies that do not exploit their workers. Much of our coffee, bananas, and chocolate products come from Equal Exchange (equalexchange.coop), a great company that strives to support small-scale farmers in Central and South America, as well as other parts of the world.

RECYCLING & COMPOSTING

As part of our respect for the environment, we work hard to reduce waste through recycling and composting. Working with Eureka Recycling, our local hauler, we have a great track record, diverting ninety-seven percent of our waste from incineration or landfills.

HANDCRAFTED QUALITY

In addition to our commitment to sustainable food practices and values, Chowgirls holds to the highest standards for the ways we handle and prepare our food.

You'll never see a corporate food wholesaler's truck pull up to our kitchen, because we don't buy prepared, packaged anything. We use whole, fresh ingredients and cook our food from scratch. Quality is also used as a measure for which ingredients we choose and the food we prepare. While we need to account for quantity in cooking for large groups, what makes Chowgirls stand out is that our food is not typical "catering" fare.

TASTE & PRESENTATION

Because our food is so fresh, it's also full-flavored, healthful, and beautiful. We regularly taste and evaluate our products in order to ensure that our guests receive the most delicious food possible. You should, too—taste your food as you cook it. Not enough salt or spice? Fix it before you serve it! Chowgirls food looks great. We keep it neat, fresh, appealing, and eye-catching. Garnishing with fresh herbs, vegetables, and fruits that represent the dish's flavor profile keeps things pretty and true.

ACCOMMODATING & APPROACHABLE

As this cookbook will demonstrate, we offer choices for eaters throughout the entire food spectrum, from meat-based to vegan dishes and gluten-free to dairy-free. We try our best to accommodate a variety of preferences and dietary restrictions for our clients' menus. Options for special-needs eaters are clearly labeled in this book and on our website. We even collaborate with customers to recreate family favorites for special occasions.

It's our goal to take comfort foods to the next level, keeping them simple while renewing them with fresh, organic ingredients and elevating their flavor profiles with our own creativity. We hope this book inspires you to revisit and share your own favorite recipes. Tweak and personalize them to your heart's content; it's fun, it's inspiring—and we built a whole company on the concept!

PHOTOS BY SARAH WHITING

A NOTE ON TERMS

(GF) Gluten-free

(DF) Dairy-free

(V) Vegetarian

(VV) Vegan

((V)) Vegetarian Option

((GF)) Gluten-free Option

SPRING

SPRING PEA TOASTS
WITH GOUDA

HONEY-RICOTTA
PROSCIUTTO CUPS

MARINATED CHÈVRE,
THREE WAYS

MINT-CRUSTED LAMB CHOPS

ASPARAGUS & CHÈVRE
POLENTA CAKES

BEEF INVOLTINI

WASABI CRAB CAKES

MISO-MAPLE SALMON WITH
BABY BOK CHOY

LEMON-ROSEMARY CHICKEN
WITH KALE CAESAR SALAD

CHICKEN & APRICOT
BASTILLA WITH ORANGE
HARISSA YOGURT

DEVILED EGGS

PIMENTO CHEESE, PEPPER
JELLY & BACON FINGER
SANDWICHES

RUMAKI

VICHYSSOISE SHOOTER

STRAWBERRY-BASIL DAIQUIRI

CHOWGIRLS BOOTLEG

RHUBARBARITA

MINT JULEP SWEET TEA

THE LIGHT AND BRIGHT FLAVORS OF SPRING PEA PURÉE COMPLEMENT THE MILD EARTHY TASTE OF GOUDA.

SPRING PEA TOASTS WITH GOUDA

Sometimes the simplest concepts are the ones that garner the most praise. This crostini recipe is a favorite of ours for spring functions. It takes almost no time to prepare, is very inexpensive, and gets regular compliments from guests for its bright flavor. For a more luxurious version, top each serving with serrano ham or prosciutto.

Preheat oven to 350°F (180°C).

Using a sharp bread knife, slice baguette on a diagonal into ¾-in (2-cm) slices. Lay slices on a baking sheet and lightly brush them with olive oil. Bake on upper oven rack for 15–20 minutes, until edges are browned and crisp but centers remain slightly soft. Remove from oven, cool slightly, and rub each slice with garlic until aromatic. Allow to cool on baking rack.

If using fresh peas, bring 4 cups water to a boil, add peas, and cook for 2–3 minutes. Drain immediately and rinse in very cold water.

In the bowl of a food processor, add garlic, tarragon, lemon juice, and cooled fresh or thawed frozen peas. Process 30–40 seconds until well blended. Add cream, lemon zest, salt, and pepper and continue to process until mixture is very smooth.

Spread a generous amount of purée on each crostini, top with Gouda, additional lemon zest, tarragon leaves, and microgreens.

Makes about 30 servings.

INGREDIENTS

1 freshly baked baguette
2 tbsp olive oil
1–2 garlic cloves
2 cups (500 mL) fresh or frozen green peas, thawed
¼ cup (60 mL) chopped fresh tarragon
2 tbsp freshly squeezed lemon juice
¼ cup (60 mL) heavy cream
2 tsp lemon zest, plus more for garnish
salt and freshly ground black pepper, to taste
4 oz (115 g) Gouda cheese, shaved into 1 ½-in (4-cm) long pieces
fresh tarragon leaves, for garnish
½ cup (125 mL) microgreens, for garnish

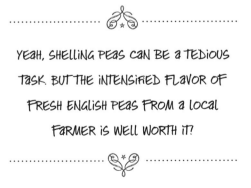

YEAH, SHELLING PEAS CAN BE A TEDIOUS TASK. BUT THE INTENSIFIED FLAVOR OF FRESH ENGLISH PEAS FROM A LOCAL FARMER IS WELL WORTH IT!

WE USE PROSCIUTTO FROM La QUERCia IN NORWaLK, IOWa. THiS FaMiLY BUSINESS SOURCES PORK FROM FaRMERS WHO PRaCTICE HiGH STaNDaRDS OF SUSTaiNaBILITY.

HONEY-RICOTTA PROSCIUTTO CUPS

Heidi was thrilled when our Northeast Minneapolis neighbors at The Lone Grazer Creamery began crafting an artisan ricotta, providing an eating experience so rich and real you can taste the farm. This unique finger food juxtaposes the fluffy texture of ricotta with crisp prosciutto and cured meat saltiness with sweet honey.

Preheat oven to 350°F (180°C).

Place a 24-cup mini muffin tin upside down on a baking sheet and coat outside of each cup with a thin layer of olive oil (1 tbsp). Wrap a slice of prosciutto around each cup, first around perimeter; then fold over onto center to finish. Ensure that edges overlap. Place in oven and bake for 20 minutes. Check color and consistency of cups. If an ashen color and still soft, return to oven and continue to bake, checking every 3–5 minutes. Prosciutto will be a deep golden-red and completely crisped when finished. Set aside to cool.

Meanwhile, make filling. In a small bowl, use a fork to beat together honey, eggs, and ricotta. Strip rosemary leaves from stems. Reserve half of the prettiest leaf clusters (at least 24) for garnish. Roughly chop remainder and fold into ricotta mixture. Set aside.

After prosciutto cups have cooled, they should easily slide off muffin tin. Remove cups and reserve on a plate or platter. Place muffin tin right-side up on baking sheet and coat inside of each cup with a thin layer of olive oil (1 tbsp). Fill each cup with ricotta mixture and bake for 15–20 minutes, until ricotta cake is firm.

Remove from oven and let cool for 30 minutes. Use a butter knife or small spatula to gently nudge each ricotta cake out of muffin tin. Set ricotta cakes into prosciutto cups. Garnish each cup with a small rosemary leaf cluster.

Makes 24 servings.

INGREDIENTS

2 tbsp olive oil, divided
24 pieces thin-sliced prosciutto
⅔ cup (80 mL) honey (preferably local)
2 eggs
2 cups (500 mL) fresh ricotta
4 sprigs fresh rosemary

SILICONE MUFFIN PANS WILL MAKE YOUR LIFE, AND THIS RECIPE, A HELLUVA LOT EASIER.

MARINATED CHÈVRE, THREE WAYS

So simple, yet so impressive, these lovely creations will keep for up to a week well-sealed in your refrigerator, becoming more delicious each day. If you'd like to make just one at a time, that's fine too, but this trio offers a little something for every guest's tastes.

MARINATED CHÈVRE WITH ROASTED TOMATOES & GARLIC

Preheat oven to 350°F (180°C).

In a medium bowl, toss tomatoes with garlic, olive oil, salt, and pepper and place on a parchment-lined baking sheet. Bake for 20 minutes. Remove from oven and gently toss. Add thyme, return to oven, and bake for 10 minutes.

Meanwhile, shape chèvre into a disc about 1 ½-in (4-cm) thick, and smooth top and sides with a spreader or butter knife.

Remove tomatoes from oven and let cool.

On a small plate or in a shallow bowl, place half the tomato mixture. Top with chèvre. Top with remainder of tomato mixture, then drizzle with 2 tbsp olive oil. Garnish with a sprig of fresh thyme. Cover and refrigerate for at least 2 hours or up to 1 week.

Makes 12 servings.

INGREDIENTS

1 cup (250 mL) halved cherry tomatoes
1 garlic clove, minced
3 tbsp olive oil (1 for roasting tomatoes, 2 for marinade)
½ tsp kosher salt
⅛ tsp freshly ground black pepper
1 tsp chopped fresh thyme leaves
4 oz (115 g) chèvre
sprig fresh thyme, for garnish

WHEN MAKING ALL THREE VERSIONS AT ONCE, USE A LARGE CHÈVRE LOG AND CUT INTO MEDALLIONS.

MARINATED CHÈVRE WITH HONEY, ROSEMARY & MARCONA ALMONDS

In a small bowl, combine rosemary with olive oil and salt.

Shape chèvre into a disc about 1 ½-in (4-cm) thick, and smooth top and sides with a spreader or butter knife.

On a small plate, drizzle half the honey and half the olive oil mixture. Center chèvre on plate and drizzle with remainder of olive oil mixture and honey. Sprinkle with almonds and a grind of black pepper. Garnish with fresh rosemary sprig. Cover and refrigerate for at least 2 hours or up to 1 week.

Makes 12 servings.

MARINATED CHÈVRE WITH WILD MUSHROOMS & ORANGE

In a large frying pan, heat olive oil on medium-low. Add garlic and shallots and sauté for 1 minute. Increase heat to high, add mushrooms, salt, and pepper. Cook, stirring continuously, for 3–5 minutes or until garlic is lightly toasted and mushrooms start to crisp. Remove from heat and drain oil into a small bowl or ramekin, then stir orange zest into oil.

Shape chèvre into a disc about 1 ½-in (4-cm) thick, and smooth top and sides with a spreader or butter knife.

In a shallow bowl, place half the mushroom mixture. Top with disc of chèvre. Add remainder of mushroom mixture, then drizzle with orange zest oil. Cover and refrigerate for at least 2 hours or up to 1 week.

Makes 12 servings.

INGREDIENTS

Marinated Chèvre with Honey, Rosemary & Marcona Almonds

1 tsp coarsely chopped rosemary leaves
3 tbsp olive oil
¼ tsp kosher salt
4 oz (115 g) chèvre
3 tbsp local honey
3 tbsp roughly chopped Marcona almonds
freshly ground black pepper, to taste
rosemary sprig, for garnish

Marinated Chèvre with Wild Mushrooms & Orange

¼ cup (60 mL) olive oil
1 garlic clove, minced
1 small shallot, minced
4 oz (115 g) cremini, porcini, shiitake, chanterelle, or other mushroom
1 tsp kosher salt
¼ tsp freshly ground black pepper
2 tsp finely minced orange zest
4 oz (115 g) chèvre

GF V

DRAGSMITH FARMS IN BARRON, WISCONSIN, IS ONE OF OUR MOST TRUSTED SOURCES FOR REGIONAL INGREDIENTS, FROM EXQUISITE MICROGREENS TO UNIQUE WATERMELON RADISHES TO PASTURE-RAISED LAMB.

MINT-CRUSTED LAMB CHOPS

Lamb is a special treat for many people, so we love to include it on many of our party menus (well, we skip it for the vegan weddings!). This recipe is a lovely match for our Chicken & Apricot Bastilla (p. 37) and also works great as a dinner entrée.

Light charcoal or gas grill, close lid, and heat to about 400°F (200°C). If using a broiler, heat to 525° F (275° C) and preheat a cast-iron frying pan.

In the bowl of a food processor, combine shallots, garlic, mint, olive oil, salt, and pepper and process until very smooth. Set aside half for garnish.

Place lamb chops on a baking sheet. Use a brush to baste tops, bottoms, and sides with half the mint purée.

Grill chops 3–4 minutes per side, until well marked and cooked to medium-rare. If broiling, place chops in preheated frying pan and broil, 2–3 in (5–8 cm) from flame for 5–6 minutes per side. Set aside on a plate and cover with aluminum foil for about 5 minutes.

When ready to serve, squeeze lemon wedge over lamb chops, drizzling juice evenly. Garnish with reserved mint purée.

Makes 10 lamb chops.

INGREDIENTS

2 tbsp diced shallots
2 small garlic cloves
½ cup (125 mL) fresh mint, plus more for garnish
2 tbsp olive oil
2 tsp salt
1 tsp freshly ground black pepper
10 lamb shoulder chops, rinsed and dried
1 large lemon wedge

THE SHORT SEASONAL AVAILABILITY OF ASPARAGUS MAKES IT AN EXTRA-SPECIAL TREAT TO ANTICIPATE EACH SPRING.

ASPARAGUS & CHÈVRE POLENTA CAKES

These bite-sized appetizers are a great way to showcase the season's finest asparagus. The creamy polenta is a nice match for it, and citrusy goat cheese (chèvre) brings on a brightness that pairs well with white wine at spring soirées.

In a medium saucepan on high heat, bring water, half and half, salt, and 1 tbsp olive oil to a boil. Whisk in cornmeal and cook over low heat for 30 minutes, stirring often, and adding additional water when mixture becomes too thick to stir. Polenta is done when smooth on the tongue with no prominent grainy feeling. Remove from heat and stir in 3 tbsp butter, mascarpone, and Parmesan until well blended.

On a parchment-lined 12 x 9-in (30 x 23-cm) baking sheet, spread polenta mixture evenly. Smooth out top and cover with plastic wrap. Gently press on surface to make plastic airtight. Refrigerate for at least 4 hours, or overnight.

When ready to make polenta cakes, remove plastic wrap and cut into 2-in (5-cm) squares.

In a large frying pan over medium, heat 2 tbsp olive oil and 1 tbsp butter. Add polenta squares and cook for 4–5 minutes on each side, until evenly browned and crispy. Set aside and allow to cool slightly.

In a large pot, steam asparagus until just tender, about 3 minutes. Rinse in ice-cold water, strain, slice in half lengthwise, and cut into 2-in (5-cm) pieces.

In a small bowl, combine chèvre, lemon zest, and chives. Top each polenta cake with a dollop of chèvre mixture and a few pieces of asparagus. Serve warm.

Makes 24 servings.

INGREDIENTS

2 cups (500 mL) water (for cooking polenta)

1 cup (250 ml) half and half

2 tsp kosher salt, plus more to taste

1 tbsp olive oil

1 cup (250 mL) course-ground cornmeal

3 tbsp unsalted butter

¼ cup (60 mL) mascarpone cheese

½ cup (125 mL) grated Parmesan or pecorino cheese

2 tbsp olive oil

1 tbsp unsalted butter

¼ lb (125 g) asparagus, woody stems removed

½ cup (125 mL) chèvre, softened

3 tsp finely chopped lemon zest

3 tsp finely chopped chives

POLENTA CAN BE MADE UP TO 2 DAYS IN ADVANCE.

GF

BEEF INVOLTINI

During her travels in Sicily, Heidi discovered a ubiquitous menu staple—involtini, in all varieties: rolls of beef, veal, swordfish, or eggplant stuffed with fillings of cheese, bread, meat, and nuts. She learned this traditional recipe, which accentuates the elusive flavor of bay leaves, from Anna Tasca Lanza's cooking school at Regaleali Vineyard in central Sicily.

STUFFING

In a medium frying pan on medium, heat olive oil. When oil is hot, add onions and sauté for 2 minutes. Add bread cubes and sauté for 2 minutes. Add ham and sauté for another minute. Remove from heat, toss in pistachios, parsley, red pepper flakes, and salt. Add mozzarella and let cool. Mix in egg, thoroughly coating stuffing. Set aside.

MEAT ROLLS

Preheat oven to 375°F (190°C).

On a parchment-lined work surface, lightly stretch beef slices, 7 at a time. Press together 2 tbsp stuffing and position on short end of beef. Leave a ½-in (1-cm) border on each side of filling, tucking in both sides of meat as you roll it up. Skewer with a toothpick. Push a bay leaf and an onion wedge onto each end of the toothpick, with the bay leaf pressed against the meat. Using a pastry brush, coat each meat roll with olive oil, then roll in breadcrumbs. Place on a parchment-lined baking sheet and bake for 15 minutes. Turn rolls and continue to bake for another 15 minutes.

Serve with lemon wedges; either whole rolls as a small plate with fork and knife, or sliced into thirds or halves as a finger food cocktail appetizer.

Makes 14 to 15 rolls.

INGREDIENTS

Stuffing
2 tbsp olive oil

¼ cup (60 mL) finely chopped onions

1 ½ cups (375 mL) ½-in (1-cm) cubes bread

½ cup (125 mL) ½-in (1-cm) cubes uncured deli ham

¼ cup (60 mL) coarsely chopped, unsalted pistachios

1 tbsp chopped fresh parsley

1 ½ tsp crushed red pepper flakes

1 tsp salt

½ cup (125 mL) ½-in (1-cm) cubes mozzarella cheese

1 egg, beaten

Meat Rolls
1 ½ lb (750 g) beef top round, cut by butcher into 3 x 5-in (8 x 12-cm) slices, ¼-in (6-mm) thick (very thin; similar to what you would use for veal scallopini)

28–30 bay leaves, fresh if possible

2 onions, sliced into 28–30 crescent-shaped wedges

2 tbsp olive oil

½ cup (125 mL) breadcrumbs

2 lemons, cut into wedges, for garnish

WASABI CRAB CAKES

These bite-sized crab cakes are a must for any Asian-themed menu. The pickled ginger garnish atop a pale-green wasabi aioli makes this one of our prettiest appetizers, elegant enough for a black-tie soirée yet approachable enough to contribute to a progressive dinner party with your neighbors.

In a medium bowl, combine crab, mayonnaise, green onions, wasabi powder, lime zest, and soy sauce and mix until well combined. Set aside.

In a separate shallow bowl or on a large plate, combine flour, salt, and pepper. In a small bowl, beat eggs and set aside. Combine breadcrumbs and sesame seeds on a large plate.

Using a tablespoon, measure even portions of crab cake mixture. Use your hands to form into small balls and line up on a parchment-lined baking sheet.

Dredge each crab cake ball, one at a time, first in flour, then eggs, and finally breadcrumb mixture. Flatten each ball into a disc on baking sheet and refrigerate until ready to deep-fry.

On high heat in a deep saucepan or deep fryer, heat oil until a candy thermometer reads 350°F (180°C). Working in small batches, fry crab cakes for 3 to 5 minutes or until lightly browned. Remove from oil and place flat onto paper towels to drain.

While crab cakes cook, combine mayonnaise with wasabi powder in a small bowl and stir well.

To serve, dollop each crab cake with about ½ tsp wasabi mayonnaise, a sliver of pickled ginger, and a tiny cucumber wedge. Serve warm.

Makes 12 to 15 pieces, depending on how much sake you drink during preparation.

INGREDIENTS

8 oz (230 g) lump crab, cleaned
½ cup (125 mL) mayonnaise
2 green onions, finely chopped
2 tsp wasabi powder
1 tsp finely chopped fresh lime zest
1 tsp soy sauce
¾ cup (175 mL) all-purpose flour
¼ tsp salt
⅛ tsp freshly ground black pepper
2 eggs, beaten
1 cup (250 mL) Panko breadcrumbs
2 tbsp black sesame seeds
2 cups (500 mL) peanut or canola oil (for frying)

Topping

¼ cup (60 mL) mayonnaise
2 tsp wasabi powder
2 tbsp pickled ginger
2 cucumber rounds, cut into eighths

PAIRS WELL WITH MISO-MAPLE SALMON
(P.33) FOR AN ASIAN-THEMED PARTY.

DF

SPRING IS THE SEASON FOR WILD-CAUGHT SALMON. TRY THIS RECIPE WITH CHINOOK OR SOCKEYE SALMON FROM THE PACIFIC NORTHWEST.

MISO-MAPLE SALMON WITH BABY BOK CHOY

A unique small plate offering, this healthful dish works wonderfully on a menu with our other Asian appetizers such as Coconut-Curry Chicken Skewers (p. 53) or Wasabi Crab Cakes (p. 31).

MISO-MAPLE GLAZE

In a small saucepan on medium heat, melt miso, syrup, and honey. When bubbling, add soy sauce, sesame oil, ginger, and orange juice and bring back to a boil. Continue to cook for 3–4 minutes, until mixture forms a glaze. Remove from heat and stir in orange zest. Set aside to cool.

SALMON

Preheat a gas or charcoal grill to medium-high and brush grate with canola oil, or preheat broiler to 525ºF (275ºC). Pat salmon dry, brush with 1 tbsp sesame oil, and season lightly with salt and pepper. Using a basting brush, lightly apply glaze to skinless side of salmon. Arrange salmon on grate, skin-side down. Cover grill and cook for about 15 minutes, basting with more sauce until salmon is firm in middle and opaque on sides. Remove from grill and keep warm. Reduce grill to medium-low heat. If broiling, place salmon skin-side down on preheated baking sheet. Place 3–4 in (8–10 cm) from flame and broil for 5–6 minutes.

BOK CHOY

Brush 1 tbsp sesame oil onto bok choy, sprinkle with salt, and place on grill. Cook, turning occasionally, for about 3 minutes each side, or until lightly charred and softened.

Cut salmon into equal portions, plate, and add bok choy to each serving. Garnish with chopped green onions and sesame seeds and serve hot or at room temperature.

Makes 12 to 16 jars.

INGREDIENTS

Miso-Maple Glaze
¼ cup (60 mL) white miso (Japanese soybean paste)
¼ cup (60 mL) real maple syrup
2 tbsp honey
2 tbsp soy sauce
2 tbsp toasted sesame oil
2 tbsp peeled and diced fresh ginger
¼ cup (60 mL) orange juice
2 tsp orange zest

Salmon
1 tbsp canola oil
3 lb (1.5 kg) fresh boneless salmon, skin-on
1 tbsp toasted sesame oil
salt and freshly ground black pepper, to taste

Bok Choy
1 tbsp toasted sesame oil
6 baby bok choy heads, halved lengthwise
1 tsp kosher salt
4 chopped green onions, green parts only, for garnish
1 tbsp mixed black and white sesame seeds, for garnish

MaKE MiSO-MaPLE GLaZE UP TO 3 DaYS iN aDVaNCE.

WE USE ORGANIC CHICKEN FROM LARRY SCHULTZ IN OWATONNA, MINNESOTA. ON THEIR WORKING FAMILY FARM, LARRY AND HIS KIDS ENSURE THAT THEIR BIRDS ENJOY A TRULY FREE-RANGE LIFESTYLE.

LEMON-ROSEMARY CHICKEN WITH KALE CAESAR SALAD

This marinated and grilled lemon-rosemary chicken has been on the Chowgirls' menu since we began our catering business and has always been a favorite wedding entrée. Here we share it as a small plate, paired with a healthful and gluten-free take on the classic Caesar salad.

CHICKEN

Rinse chicken under cold water and pat dry. Place in a medium-sized bowl with olive oil, lemon juice and zest, garlic, rosemary, salt, and pepper. Stir to combine all ingredients, making sure that chicken is well coated. Cover bowl, or transfer to a resealable plastic bag and refrigerate for at least 3 hours.

Heat a charcoal or gas grill to 350°F (180°C) and spray grate with nonstick cooking oil. If using a broiler, preheat to 525°F (275°C). Grill chicken thighs, about 10 minutes each side, until well marked and cooked through. If broiling, place chicken thighs on lightly oiled broiler pan. Broil 4–6 in (10 to 15 cm) from flame for 10–15 minutes each side. Allow to rest for 5 minutes, then cut chicken on a diagonal into ¾-in (2-cm) strips.

SALAD

Rinse and dry kale and place in a large bowl. In a small bowl, whisk together olive oil, vinegar, anchovy paste, egg yolk, garlic powder, salt, and pepper. Continue whisking until dressing has thickened.

Drizzle dressing over kale and, using your hands, rub leaves until well coated. Set aside at room temperature and allow to rest for at least 1 hour to ensure that kale is tender and easy to chew. Before serving, add chopped almonds and Parmesan cheese.

To serve, spoon about ¼ cup (60 mL) salad onto each small plate, then top with 1 or 2 chicken strips.

Makes 12 small plates.

INGREDIENTS

Chicken

6 boneless, skinless chicken thighs (about 2 lb/900 g), cut in half
3 tbsp olive oil
2 tbsp freshly squeezed lemon juice
3 tsp lemon zest
1 tbsp minced garlic
1 tbsp chopped rosemary
1 ½ tsp kosher salt
½ tsp freshly ground black pepper

Salad

1 bunch kale, stems removed, chopped into ½-in (1-cm) strips
⅓ cup (80 mL) olive oil
3 tbsp white wine vinegar
1 tsp anchovy paste (optional)
1 egg yolk
¼ tsp garlic powder
kosher salt and freshly ground pepper, to taste
½ cup (125 mL) sliced almonds, chopped
¼ cup (60 mL) grated Parmesan cheese

ALMONDS AND APRICOTS GIVE THIS BEAUTIFUL
SAVORY APPETIZER A UNIQUE TEXTURE AND FLAVOR.

CHICKEN & APRICOT BASTILLA WITH ORANGE HARISSA YOGURT

When tasked with creating a Moroccan-themed menu for a client in 2009, Amy crafted this sweet and savory pastry triangle. Based loosely on a delicacy with pigeon meat as its primary protein, this version, substituting chicken breast, has been a hit at parties ever since.

CHICKEN & APRICOT BASTILLA

Preheat oven to 375°F (190°C).

In a large frying pan, heat olive oil and sauté onions and garlic for about 3 minutes. Add chicken, salt, and pepper, and continue to sauté about 7 minutes, until chicken is cooked through.

In a food processor, pulse together chicken, apricots, almonds, and cinnamon, about 12 times, until all ingredients are well chopped and combined. Set filling aside.

Unroll phyllo sheets, then cover with a damp towel to prevent drying. Place single sheet of phyllo on a cutting board and brush lightly with melted butter. Top with another sheet and, again, brush with butter. Cut long edge of layered phyllo into 5 strips, roughly 3-in (8-cm) wide. Place 1 tbsp filling about 1 in (2.5 cm) from bottom of each strip, then fold corner diagonally across to opposite edge, forming a triangle. Continue to fold triangle onto itself, all the way to the end of the strip, then brush top of triangle with butter. Make more triangles in the same fashion until all filling has been used.

On a parchment-lined baking sheet, bake phyllo triangles, seam side down, for 20–25 minutes, until golden brown.

Serve bastilla warm or at room temperature with Orange-Harissa Yogurt for dipping.

Makes 24 to 30 pieces.

ORANGE HARISSA YOGURT

In a small bowl, combine yogurt, orange juice and zest, and harissa.

INGREDIENTS

3 tbsp olive oil
1 medium onion, diced
3 garlic cloves, minced
1 lb (500 g) chicken breast, finely chopped
2 tsp kosher salt
1 tsp freshly ground black pepper
1 cup (250 mL) chopped dried apricots
1 cup (250 mL) sliced almonds, toasted
  and chopped
1 tsp ground cinnamon
1 16-oz (500-g) package phyllo dough
¼ cup (60 mL) butter, melted

Orange Harissa Yogurt

1 cup (60 mL) plain Greek yogurt
juice and zest of 1 orange
1–2 tsp harissa (to taste)

TO GET THE MOST OUT OF YOUR CITRUS, ALWAYS ZEST YOUR FRUIT BEFORE JUICING IT.

DEVILED EGGS

This traditional picnic side dish has been making a comeback as a trendy and versatile appetizer, especially with our variations. Good thing Chowgirl Amy has a wicked master recipe! We get constant raves on these—and often hear that they're "the best deviled eggs I've ever had!"

Fill a large saucepan with cold water and add eggs. Bring to a boil on high heat and boil eggs for 7 minutes. Remove from heat and let sit for 10 minutes. Drain eggs and rinse in cold water. Peel and slice each egg in half. (Rinse and wipe knife between each egg to ensure a clean slice.)

Scoop out egg yolks and add to a food processor. Place egg white halves on a deviled egg plate or flat surface and set aside. Pulse yolks about 12 times, until crumbly. Add remainder of ingredients and process until smooth, about 20 seconds. Scrape down sides of bowl and process for 10 seconds.

Using a spatula, transfer mixture to a piping bag. Using your hands, push all the filling to one corner and press out any air.

Pipe mixture into egg white halves, about 1 tbsp per half.

Makes 24 eggs.

VARIATIONS

Bright & Spicy Deviled Eggs
In yolk mixture, replace mustard with 1 tbsp Sriracha sauce. Top with chopped fresh cilantro and black sesame seeds.

Curried Deviled Eggs
Add 1 tsp mild sweet curry powder to yolk mixture. Make it over the top with ½ tsp mango chutney on each egg.

Tarragon Deviled Eggs
Add 1 tbsp finely chopped fresh tarragon and ½ tsp tarragon vinegar to yolk mixture. Garnish with tarragon leaves.

INGREDIENTS

12 eggs
¼ tsp salt
½ cup (125 mL) mayonnaise
¼ cup (60 mL) sour cream
¼ tsp garlic powder
1 tsp Dijon or grainy brown mustard

IF YOU DON'T HAVE A PIPING BAG, DON'T SWEAT IT? SIMPLY FILL A QUART-SIZED RESEALABLE BAG, SNIP OFF A BOTTOM CORNER, AND YOU'RE GOOD TO GO.

MOVE OVER, GRANDMA, THERE ARE A FEW NEW DEVILED EGG RECIPES IN TOWN!

PIMENTO CHEESE, PEPPER JELLY & BACON FINGER SANDWICHES

A staple of the American South, pimento cheese is making a comeback. This finger sandwich makes wonderful use of the spread, pairing it with a sweet and spicy pepper jelly and salty crisp bacon, taking "grilled cheese" to the next level! Eliminate bacon for a vegetarian appetizer

PIMENTO CHEESE

In a food processor, combine cream cheese and mayonnaise and process until smooth. Add cheeses, garlic powder, Worcestershire and Tabasco sauce, salt, and pepper. Pulse 15 times or until all ingredients are well blended. Transfer to a medium bowl and stir in pimentos.

SANDWICHES

To prepare each sandwich: Spread about 2 tbsp pimento cheese onto each of 16 bread slices. Spread about 1 tbsp pepper jelly onto each of remaining 16 slices and top jelly with 2 bacon pieces.

Press cheese and jelly slices together gently to form 16 sandwiches.

Spread a light coating of butter on the outside of each sandwich.

Heat a large griddle on medium-high until just smoking, then reduce heat to medium-low. Lightly toast each sandwich, about 1 minute per side, until browned. Remove from heat. Using a sharp knife, remove crusts, then cut each sandwich into 2 triangular segments. Serve warm.

Makes 32 finger sandwiches.

INGREDIENTS

Pimento Cheese
4 oz (115 g) cream cheese, room
   temperature
½ cup (125 mL) mayonnaise
8 oz (230 g) sharp cheddar cheese,
   shredded
8 oz (230g) Gouda cheese, shredded
¼ tsp garlic powder
1 tsp Worcestershire sauce
dash Tabasco sauce
1 tsp kosher salt
½ tsp freshly ground black pepper
½ cup (125 mL) pimentos or roasted red
   peppers, finely diced

Sandwiches
1 16-oz (500-g) loaf thinly sliced white
   sandwich bread, about 32 slices
4 oz (115 g) pepper jelly
1 lb (500 g) bacon, cooked crisp, strips cut
   in half lengthwise
¼ cup (60 mL) butter, softened

MAKE PIMENTO CHEESE UP TO 3 DAYS IN ADVANCE. JUST BE CAREFUL NOT TO DEVOUR IT BEFORE YOU MAKE THESE AMAZING SANDWICHES.

(v)

RUMAKI

Rumaki, a classic appetizer from the 1960s cocktail-party era, was traditionally made with soy sauce, bacon, ginger, and whole chicken livers. Heidi's grandmother, a caterer during that decade, served a more accessible version, replacing the chicken livers with whole water chestnuts. Our recipe allows your guests to choose between a water chestnut or a sweet, chewy date—or one or two of each—as they are virtually irresistible.

RUMAKI

Preheat oven to 350°F (180°C).

Allow cut bacon to warm to room temperature; warm bacon is easier to stretch around water chestnuts and dates. Wrap bacon slices around individual water chestnuts or dates, skewering each with a sturdy toothpick. Place dates and chestnuts on separate parchment-lined baking sheets ½-in (1-cm) apart. Bake dates for 30 minutes and water chestnuts for 45 minutes or until bacon is crisped.

GLAZE

While bacon is working its magic in the oven, in a medium saucepan whisk together remainder of ingredients. Simmer on low heat until mixture bubbles and reaches a deep red color, about 15 minutes. Remove from heat and pour half into a shallow baking dish and half into a small bowl. Dip each rumaki piece into bowl of glaze, then transfer to baking dish. Bake at 350°F (180°C) for another 20 minutes, platter, and serve hot.

Makes 45 pieces.

INGREDIENTS

Rumaki

1 lb (500 g) bacon, sliced into thirds
1 8-oz (228 mL) can whole water chestnuts
25 whole pitted dates

Glaze

½ cup (160 mL) tomato paste
¼ cup (125 mL) water
¾ cup (175 mL) firmly packed brown sugar
1 tbsp onion powder
½ tsp garlic granules
1 tsp chili powder
1 tsp kosher salt
1 tsp Worcestershire sauce
⅛ tsp ground allspice
¼ tsp ground cloves
½ tsp red pepper flakes
¾ cup (250 mL) mayonnaise
½ cup (125 mL) freshly squeezed orange juice
¼ cup (60 mL) rice vinegar
1 tbsp grated fresh ginger

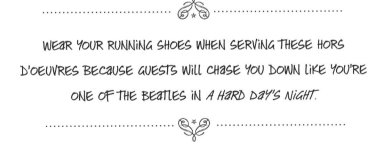

WEAR YOUR RUNNING SHOES WHEN SERVING THESE HORS D'OEUVRES BECAUSE GUESTS WILL CHASE YOU DOWN LIKE YOU'RE ONE OF THE BEATLES IN *A HARD DAY'S NIGHT*.

VICHYSSOISE SHOOTER

This cold potato-leek soup is one of our simplest recipes, with only 4 core ingredients. We love putting this out as a starter on a spring or summer luncheon table—it's just a sip, but the silky texture and burst of flavors really impress guests!

In a large stock pot on medium heat, combine leeks, potatoes, stock, salt, and pepper. Bring to a boil, cover, and cook for 45 minutes or until leeks and potatoes are tender. Allow to cool slightly, then, working in batches, purée mixture using a blender, food processor, or immersion blender. (Be careful when working with hot liquids.) In batches, pour through a sieve to remove solids. Return liquid to pot and bring back to a boil.

Remove from heat, mix in cream, and pour into chilled shot glasses using a glass measuring cup with a pour spout. Garnish with fresh minced herbs. Refrigerate for at least 2 hours, until very cold. Serve cold.

Makes 24 to 30 shots.

INGREDIENTS

4 cups (1 L) leeks (white parts only)

4 cups (1 L) peeled and sliced russet or other large potatoes

3 quarts (3 L) chicken stock

3 tsp salt

1 ½ tsp ground white pepper

¾ cup (175 mL) heavy cream

3 tbsp minced fresh tarragon, chives, or other savory herb, for garnish

WE FEEL THAT THE CHICKEN STOCK REALLY TAKES THIS RECIPE TO ANOTHER LEVEL, BUT YOU CAN EASILY MAKE IT VEGETARIAN BY SUBSTITUTING VEGETABLE STOCK.

(GF) (V)

STRAWBERRY-BASIL DAIQUIRI

We love to use fresh fruits and herbs in our drink mixes—it's one of the ways we stay true to our dedication to seasonal ingredients. We keep it simple, making hand-crafted cocktails that don't need a lot of mixology performance—the ingredients are the stars.

DAIQUIRI

In a glass pitcher, mix together all ingredients except garnishes. Just before serving, pour into a cocktail shaker with ice and shake for 8 to 10 seconds. Strain into coupe glasses. Garnish each with a floating strawberry slice and basil leaf.

Makes 12 cocktails.

STRAWBERRY-BASIL SIMPLE SYRUP

In a medium-sized saucepan on high heat, bring strawberries to a boil in 2 cups (500 mL) water. Reduce heat to medium and simmer for 20 minutes, skimming off foam as needed.

Into a medium-sized bowl, pour mixture through a fine mesh strainer. Do not press strawberries to get out extra liquid as it will fog the syrup. Instead, allow to drain for at least 10 minutes before discarding strawberry solids.

Submerge basil leaves in strawberry liquid and allow to rest for 1 hour. Strain back into saucepan. On high heat, bring mixture to a boil, add sugar, and stir until sugar is completely dissolved. Reduce heat to low and simmer for 5 minutes. Remove from heat and allow to cool completely.

Makes 1 ½ cups (375 mL).

INGREDIENTS

Daiquiri

3 cups (700 mL) white rum

1 ½ cups (375 mL) freshly squeezed lime juice, strained

1 ½ cups (375 mL) Strawberry-Basil Simple Syrup (recipe below)

3 strawberries, cut into 4 slices each, for garnish

12 small unblemished basil leaves, for garnish

Strawberry-Basil Simple Syrup

1 lb (500 g) organic strawberries, hulled and quartered

½ cup (125 mL) basil leaves, tightly packed

1 cup (250 mL) sugar

IT'S BEEN CLAIMED THAT MINNESOTA'S NATIVE SON, AUTHOR F. SCOTT FITZGERALD, WAS A BOOTLEG ENTHUSIAST.

CHOWGIRLS BOOTLEG

This refreshing drink is known as the signature cocktail of the Minnesota country-club set. Local honey is the preferred sweetener, but agave syrup is a nice, clean alternative.

In a blender, process lemon and lime juice, honey, and mint leaves until smooth. Add 1 cup ice and continue to blend until all ingredients are incorporated.

Into each highball glass, pour 2 oz (60 mL) gin over ice. Add 2 oz (60 mL) mixer and 2 oz (60 mL) club soda. Stir. Garnish with fresh mint.

Makes 8 cocktails.

INGREDIENTS

1 ½ cups (375 mL) freshly squeezed lemon juice
¾ cup (175 mL) lime juice
¾ cup (175 mL) honey (preferably local), slightly warmed, or agave syrup
1 cup (250 mL) fresh mint leaves, tightly packed
1 cup (250 mL) ice, plus more for glasses
2 cups (500 mL) gin
2 cups (500 mL) club soda
fresh mint leaves, for garnish

RHUBARB + MARGARITA = RHUBARBARITA

RHUBARBARITA

One of the most promising signs of warm weather to come is the large green leaves and pink stalks of the rhubarb plant. Usually tamed by a strawberry accompaniment, rhubarb's tart and tangy flavor—and its gorgeous color—is highlighted in this fun cocktail.

RHUBARBARITA

Juice 1 lime into a shallow, wide bowl. Slice other lime into rounds. Dip rims of margarita glass first in lime juice and then in coarse sugar. Fill glasses with ice. In a cocktail shaker, shake together equal amounts of rhubarb syrup and tequila, pour into glasses, and garnish with lime slice.

Makes 6 to 8 cocktails.

RHUBARB SYRUP

In a medium pot on high heat, bring rhubarb and 3 cups (1 L) water to a rolling boil. Reduce heat and simmer for 45 minutes or until rhubarb is completely cooked and dissolved into threads. Strain through a fine-mesh sieve into a bowl and pour liquid back into pot. Return to stove and bring to a boil, reducing liquid by half. Stir in sugar until completely dissolved. Allow to cool.

Makes 2 cups.

INGREDIENTS

Rhubarbarita
2 limes
½ cup (125 mL) coarse sugar crystals
26-oz (750-mL) bottle silver tequila

Rhubarb Syrup
1 lb (500 g) rhubarb stalks, chopped into 1-in (2.5-cm) pieces
1 cup (250 mL) sugar

PEOPLE are OFTEN VERY GENEROUS WHEN GiViNG away RHUBaRB. GRaCiOUSLY aCCEPT EVERY OFFERiNG aND STOCK YOUR FREEZER FULL OF THiS SYRUP SO YOU CaN RELiSH iT aNY TiME OF THE YEaR.

MINT JULEP SWEET TEA

The traditional mint julep, while growing in popularity alongside other Southern US staples, isn't exactly everyone's "cup of tea." It's a boozy, straightforward whiskey drink that's too strong for some palates. This more approachable variation is sweet, sour, and perfect for Kentucky Derby parties!

Bring 3 cups (700 mL) water to a boil and remove from heat. Add tea bags and let steep for 5 minutes.

Remove tea bags, bring tea to a boil, then stir in brown sugar until dissolved. Continue to cook for about 10 minutes until liquid is reduced by half. Remove from heat. Cool slightly and add bourbon and lemon juice.

Place fresh mint in a medium bowl. Pour warm bourbon mixture over mint. Cover and refrigerate for 30–60 minutes.

When ready to serve, strain liquid into a cocktail pitcher and add club soda. Serve over ice in tall iced tea glasses, garnished with fresh lemon wedges.

Makes 6 glasses.

INGREDIENTS

3 mint tea bags
3 black or Earl Grey tea bags
1 cup (250 mL) brown sugar
1 ½ cups (375 mL) bourbon
juice of 1 lemon
½ cup (125 mL) fresh mint, muddled
2 cups (500 mL) club soda or seltzer
6 lemon wedges, for garnish

SUMMER

ZUCCHINI FRITTERS WITH
SUCCOTASH SALAD

GUACAMOLE &
PICO DE GALLO

COCONUT-CURRY CHICKEN
SKEWERS WITH SESAME
PEANUT SAUCE

GAZPACHO JARS

FLANK STEAK SKEWERS WITH
CHIMICHURRI

CORN PUDDING WITH TOMATO
& BASIL SALAD

MANGO CHICKEN SALAD

BIG WOODS BLUE CANAPÉS

HEIRLOOM TOMATO TARTLETS

THREE SUMMER BRUSCHETTAS

SWEET CORN RISOTTO
WITH SHRIMP

LAMB MEATBALLS WITH SPICED
YOGURT CHUTNEY

CARPACCIO & GREEN BEAN
BUNDLES

BABY HOT BROWNS

BENEDICTINE FINGER
SANDWICHES

SUMMER SHRUBS

WHITE SANGRIA

SUMMER THYME

ANOTHER GREAT USE
FOR SUMMER'S MOST
UBIQUITOUS VEGETABLE.

ZUCCHINI FRITTERS WITH SUCCOTASH SALAD

This is a great appetizer for those weeks when summer squash is in full season, often to the point that we have more than we need. Topped with a fresh salad made from some of summer's other favorite bumper crops, these crispy fritters are a star for parties or a light dinner.

FRITTERS

In a colander, sprinkle zucchini with salt and toss well. Set colander over a towel and let drain for 10 minutes. In the meantime, in a large bowl whisk together flour, cornstarch, pepper, and garlic powder. Add eggs, basil, and shallots and stir until well combined.

Using a clean dishtowel, wring zucchini dry, then add to flour and egg mixture. Stir to incorporate well.

Heat oil in a large frying pan on medium heat. Working in batches, drop zucchini mixture by tablespoonful into hot oil. Flatten slightly, then cook until golden and crisp, about 2 minutes per side. Drain fritters on paper towel on a plate and keep warm.

SALAD

In a medium frying pan on medium heat, melt butter. Add corn, bell peppers, and green onions and sauté for 3–5 minutes. Season with lemon juice, salt, and pepper.

To assemble, plate each fritter and garnish with about 2 tsp crème fraîche and 1 tbsp succotash. Garnish with more fresh basil, if desired.

Makes 24 to 30 fritters.

INGREDIENTS

Fritters
2 lb (900 g) zucchini, grated
1 tsp kosher salt
⅓ cup (80 mL) all-purpose flour
2 tbsp cornstarch
½ tsp freshly ground black pepper
¼ tsp garlic powder
2 eggs, beaten
2 tbsp finely chopped basil
2 tbsp finely diced shallots
½ cup (125 mL) sunflower or other light
    vegetable oil

Salad
2 tbsp butter
2 ears fresh sweet corn, kernels removed
⅓ cup (80 mL) diced red bell pepper
3 green onions, white and green parts,
    chopped
2 tsp freshly squeezed lemon juice
½ tsp kosher salt
¼ tsp freshly ground black pepper
1 cup (250 mL) crème fraîche
chopped fresh basil (optional), for garnish

(v)

GUACAMOLE & PICO DE GALLO

Guacamole and salsa are perhaps the most common guests at any casual party. Easily purchased with bagged chips at the grocery store, most are ho-hum with predictable flavor profiles. Years ago, we discovered there was a perfect method to make both from scratch. Summertime in-season tomatoes are a must!

GUACAMOLE

In a food processor, combine garlic, onions, cilantro, oil, salt, and pepper and process for 30–40 seconds or until a smooth paste forms. Add chopped avocado and purée until very smooth. Add lime juice and taste. Adjust seasoning. Transfer to a bowl and serve with Pico De Gallo and tortilla chips.

Makes 1 quart (1 L).

PICO DE GALLO

Mix all ingredients together in a medium bowl to combine well, and serve with guacamole and tortilla chips. May be stored in refrigerator for up to 3 days.

Makes 1 quart (1 L).

INGREDIENTS

Guacamole
1 fresh garlic clove, peeled and chopped
½ cup (125 mL) chopped white onions
¼ cup (60 mL) coarsely chopped fresh cilantro leaves
2 tbsp olive oil
1 ½ tsp kosher salt
1 tsp freshly ground black pepper
8 ripe avocadoes, pitted, skins removed, roughly chopped
2 tbsp freshly squeezed lime juice

Pico de Gallo
8 Roma tomatoes, seeded and chopped
3 garlic cloves, peeled and finely chopped
½ cup (125 mL) diced white onions
¼ cup (60 mL) chopped fresh cilantro leaves
1 jalapeño pepper, stem, seeds, and pith removed, diced
1 ½ tsp kosher salt
1 tsp freshly ground black pepper
2 tbsp olive oil
2 tbsp freshly squeezed lemon juice

YOU KNOW WHAT WOULD REALLY IMPRESS YOUR FRIENDS? IF YOU CUT UP SOME CORN TORTILLA SHELLS AND FRIED THOSE BABIES TO MAKE HOMEMADE CHIPS! WE SUGGEST USING LIGHT OLIVE OIL, ABOUT 2-IN (5-CM) DEEP, HEATED TO 325°F (160°C), FOR 5–6 MINUTES PER BATCH.

(V) (DF) (GF)

COCONUT-CURRY CHICKEN SKEWERS WITH SESAME PEANUT SAUCE

This Thai appetizer has become a staple of catering companies and home entertainers everywhere, but we think our recipe is one of the best. A long marinade (we recommend overnight) will ensure not only a nice bright gold color but the rich coconut and curry flavor profile that we love.

CHICKEN SKEWERS

In a large bowl, whisk together all ingredients except chicken. Add chicken, cover, and marinate, refrigerated, for at least 4 hours or overnight.

Soak at least 24 10-in (25-cm) wooden skewers in tap water for 30 minutes or more. This will prevent them from burning over flames.

Preheat a gas or charcoal grill to medium heat. If using a broiler, preheat to 525ºF (275ºC) and preheat a baking sheet or broiler pan. Skewer each chicken cube on a pre-soaked skewer and cook, uncovered, on grill for 3–4 minutes each side, until nicely marked and cooked through. If broiling, placed skewered chicken on preheated baking sheet, 3–4 in (8–10 cm) from flame. Cook for 5–6 minutes. Serve hot or at room temperature with sliced cucumbers and Sesame Peanut Sauce.

Makes 24 skewers.

SESAME PEANUT SAUCE

In a large frying pan on medium, heat sesame and olive oils. Add shallots, ginger, and garlic, and cook until softened, about 3 minutes. Add rice wine and bring to a boil. Cook for 1 minute more, then add remainder of ingredients, stirring until well combined. If mixture is too thick, add up to ½ cup (125 mL) warm water until desired consistency is reached.

Makes 1 cup (250 mL).

INGREDIENTS

Chicken Skewers

1 17.5-oz (518-mL) can coconut milk
¼ cup (60 mL) lime juice
2 tbsp mild curry powder
2 tbsp fish sauce
2 tbsp white sugar
2 tsp sesame oil
2 tsp salt
1 tbsp peeled and minced fresh ginger
3 garlic cloves, peeled and minced
4 boneless, skinless chicken breasts
    (about 1 lb [500 g]), cut into 1-in (2.5-cm)
    cubes

Sesame Peanut Sauce

2 tsp sesame oil
2 tsp olive oil
2 shallots, diced
2 tsp peeled and chopped fresh ginger
1 garlic clove, peeled and minced
¼ cup (60 mL) rice wine
1 tbsp soy sauce
¼ cup (60 mL) brown sugar
2 tbsp tahini
¼ cup (60 mL) peanut butter
2 tbsp ketchup
2 tsp lime juice
½ tsp red pepper flakes
½ tsp salt

GUESTS ARE NATURALLY DRAWN
TO THIS FUN PRESENTATION OF A
SUMMER CLASSIC.

GAZPACHO JARS

Ideal for outdoor summer parties, this fresh chilled soup is the perfect way to show off beautiful heirloom tomatoes and cucumbers, whether they're homegrown or picked up at your local farmers' market that morning! Refreshing and cool, this might be the best gazpacho you've ever tasted.

In a food processor, pulse chopped tomatoes about 10 times. Transfer to a large bowl. Add bell peppers and cucumbers to food processor and repeat, pulsing until vegetables are coarsely chopped but not puréed. Transfer to bowl with tomatoes. Add onions and garlic to food processor and pulse about 10 times. Add to tomato mixture. Stir in tomato juice, olive oil, vinegar, lemon juice, salt, pepper, and dill and combine well.

Transfer soup to 4-oz (114-mL) canning jars, seal, and refrigerate for 2 hours or up to 3 days.

Serve chilled. And don't forget to serve with a spoon!

Makes 12 to 16 jars.

INGREDIENTS

- 2 cups (500 mL) roughly chopped tomatoes
- 1 cup (250 mL) roughly chopped yellow bell peppers
- 1 cup (250 mL) roughly chopped cucumbers
- ½ cup (125 mL) roughly chopped white onions
- 4 garlic cloves, peeled and chopped
- 6 cups (1.5 L) tomato juice
- ⅓ cup (80 mL) olive oil
- ¼ cup (60 mL) red wine vinegar
- 3 tbsp lemon juice
- 1 tbsp kosher salt
- 1 tsp freshly ground black pepper
- 1 tbsp chopped fresh dill

IF YOU'RE REALLY AMBITIOUS, DOLL UP THE LIDS WITH FANCY PAPER OR FABRIC.

VV · DF · GF

FLANK STEAK SKEWERS WITH CHIMICHURRI

In our formative years, we captured the attention of celebrity chef Andrew Zimmern before he hit the big time with Travel Channel's *Bizarre Foods*. He profiled Chowgirls in a local TV news segment and hired us to assist at special events, including his wife's birthday party. We fell in love with his chimichurri sauce and are thankful that Andrew has graciously shared his recipe with us and, in turn, you.

STEAK

Pat steak with paper towel to remove excess moisture.

In a small bowl, combine salt, pepper, garlic powder, oregano, and cayenne to create a dry rub for steak. Rub top, bottom, and sides of steak with spice mixture and set aside, allowing it to come to room temperature.

Heat a gas or charcoal grill to 350°F (180°C). If using a broiler, preheat to 525°F (275°C) and preheat a cast-iron frying pan. Baste steak with olive oil. Grill steak, covered, for 6–7 minutes, then turn and grill for another 6–7 minutes (for medium-rare.) If broiling, place steak in preheated frying pan and broil 2–3 in (5–8 cm) from flame for 2–3 minutes per side. Set aside and allow to rest at least 15 minutes before slicing. Slice ¼-in (6-mm) thick, against the grain, on a diagonal, and skewer slices with 8-in (20-cm) bamboo skewers. Serve with chimichurri.

Makes 24 skewers.

CHIMICHURRI

In a food processor or blender, combine parsley, cilantro, oregano, bay leaves, garlic, chile, and cumin, and process until finely chopped. Add olive oil and vinegar and pulse to combine. Season with salt.

Makes 1 cup (250 mL).

INGREDIENTS

Steak
1 ½ lb (750 g) flank steak
1 tbsp kosher salt
1 tbsp freshly ground black pepper
2 tsp garlic powder
1 tbsp dried oregano
⅛ tsp cayenne pepper
2 tbsp olive oil

Chimichurri
1 cup (250 mL) loosely packed flat-leaf parsley
¼ cup (60 mL) loosely packed cilantro
3 tbsp fresh oregano leaves
2 fresh bay leaves
2 garlic cloves, peeled
1 serrano chile, stemmed, seeded, and coarsely chopped
½ tsp ground cumin
¼ cup (60 mL) plus 2 tbsp olive oil
2 tbsp red wine vinegar
kosher salt, to taste

WE USE GRASS-FED BEEF FOR OUR FLANK STEAK SKEWERS. OUR FAVORITE REGIONAL SUPPLIER IS THOUSAND HILLS CATTLE CO.

CORN PUDDING WITH TOMATO & BASIL SALAD

We love it when Amy's Kentucky accent flares up, especially on our menu. This creamy savory pudding features everyone's favorite summer flavors—corn, tomato, and basil. Its bright taste and colors are perfectly in tune with any summer party.

PUDDING

Preheat oven to 350°F (180°C).

In a food processor, combine 1 cup (250 mL) corn, shallots, and cream and purée for 10 seconds, until well blended. Transfer mixture to a large bowl and add remaining corn, dill, tarragon, salt, pepper, eggs, and cheese. Mix well.

Pour batter into a buttered 2-qt (2-L) casserole dish and cover loosely with aluminum foil. Set casserole into a 1-in (2.5-cm) water bath and bake for 40 minutes. Remove aluminum foil and bake an additional 20 minutes. Remove from water bath and cool slightly.

SALAD

In a medium bowl, mix all salad ingredients until well blended. Chill until ready for use.

Serve ½ cup (125 mL) corn pudding on a small plate with ¼ cup (60 mL) Tomato & Basil Salad.

Makes 12 to 16 servings.

INGREDIENTS

Pudding

3 cups (700 mL) fresh or frozen corn kernels, thawed
2 shallots, diced
1 cup (250 mL) heavy whipping cream
1 tbsp chopped fresh dill
1 tbsp chopped fresh tarragon
1 ½ tsp salt
½ tsp freshly ground black pepper
6 eggs, beaten
1 cup grated white cheddar cheese

Salad

3 medium heirloom or other fresh tomatoes, finely chopped
¼ cup (60 mL) basil chiffonade
1 tbsp extra virgin olive oil
1 tsp white balsamic vinegar
2 tsp lemon zest
½ tsp salt
freshly ground black pepper, to taste

MANGO CHICKEN SALAD

This recipe dates back to the earliest days of Chowgirls and is still a favorite of our regular and new customers alike. The addition of fresh ripe mango gives this salad an unexpected tang while the crunchy almonds create great texture. Serve on slider buns, miniature croissants, or in fresh, crisp Belgian endive leaves for a lighter presentation.

Preheat oven to 350°F (180°C).

Rinse and dry chicken breasts, then brush both sides with olive oil. Sprinkle with salt and pepper and place on a large baking sheet. Bake for 25–30 minutes or until cooked through. Remove from baking sheet and let cool. When cooled, coarsely chop chicken and place in a medium bowl. Add mango, almonds, green onions, and cilantro and toss well.

To make dressing, mix all ingredients in a medium bowl and stir until well combined. Pour dressing over chicken and stir until fully incorporated.

Makes about 1 quart (1 L).

Fills 16 mini croissants or 32 endive leaves.

INGREDIENTS

4 boneless, skinless chicken breasts
2 tsp olive oil
1 tsp kosher salt
½ tsp freshly ground pepper
1 mango, peeled, pitted, and diced
½ cup (125 mL) sliced almonds
4 green onions, white and green parts, chopped
¼ cup (60 mL) chopped fresh cilantro

Dressing
¾ cup (175 mL) mayonnaise
½ cup (125 mL) Greek yogurt
3 tbsp mango chutney
2 tsp Dijon mustard
1 tsp minced garlic
2 tsp minced fresh ginger
1 ½ tsp mild curry powder
2 tsp soy sauce
2 tsp lime juice
½ tsp Sriracha sauce (optional)
1 tsp kosher salt
½ tsp freshly ground black pepper

WE ARE SO SMITTEN WITH SHEPHERD'S WAY
UNIQUE SHEEP'S MILK BLUE CHEESE THAT MAARI,
CHOWGIRLS' JANE-OF-ALL-TRADES, CREATED THIS
DELICIOUSLY DISTINCT FINGER FOOD.

BIG WOODS BLUE CANAPÉS

One of our most popular finger foods, Big Woods Blue Canapés came to us by way of a family farm in Nerstrand, Minnesota. Shepherd's Way produces some of the best sheep's milk cheeses in the Midwest. Try this recipe with a blue cheese that's regional to you—it's an excellent choice for any wine-centric event!

WINE BISCUITS

In a food processor, combine all dry ingredients. Add butter in small chunks, pulsing after each addition, until mixture resembles coarse meal. Add wine a little bit at a time, and pulse until dough comes together as a loose ball. Do not over-mix. Transfer dough to a floured surface and roll into a 1-in (2.5-cm) wide log. Cover in plastic wrap and place in freezer. Allow to rest in freezer for at least 4 hours, as this will make it easier to cut into rounds. Preheat oven to 325°F (160°C).

Keeping dough very cold, cut into ½-in (1-cm) thick rounds. Place rounds 1-in (2.5-cm) apart on a parchment-lined baking sheet. Bake for 20–25 minutes, rotating sheet halfway through, until biscuits are slightly browned and firm in the middle. Remove from sheet and transfer biscuits to a baking rack and let cool.

TOPPING

Preheat oven to 325°F (160°C).

In a bowl, toss grapes with olive oil, salt, and pepper, then transfer to a parchment-lined baking sheet. Bake for 30–40 minutes, tossing them halfway through, until lightly caramelized. Remove grapes from oven and let cool to room temperature.

To prepare the canapés: Top each biscuit with 1 tsp blue cheese, a roasted grape, and an almond. Place on a serving platter and drizzle each canapé with honey. Sprinkle very lightly with lavender buds and serve at room temperature.

Makes 30 to 32 canapés.

INGREDIENTS

Wine Biscuits

1 cup (250 mL) all-purpose flour
¼ cup (60 mL) sugar
1 tsp baking powder
1 tsp salt
¼ tsp freshly ground black pepper
3 tbsp butter, softened
¼ cup (60 mL) white wine

Topping

¾ lb (375 g) red grapes
1 tbsp olive oil
salt and freshly ground black pepper, to taste
4 oz (115 g) blue cheese, room temperature
¾ cup (175 mL) Marcona almonds
3 tbsp honey (preferably local)
1 tbsp dried lavender buds

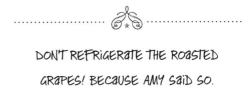

DON'T REFRIGERATE THE ROASTED GRAPES! BECAUSE AMY SAID SO.

HEIRLOOM TOMATO TARTLETS

With the exquisite presentation for this recipe, it's worth the extra effort to go out of your way for heirloom cherry tomatoes. And be on the lookout for a regional ricotta; artisanal cheeses always offer a top quality eating experience.

Preheat oven to 350°F (180°C).

In a medium bowl, whisk together ricotta, ¾ cup cheese, eggs, and chopped basil. Season with salt and pepper and whisk until combined.

Butter each cup of a mini muffin tin and gently press a round of pastry dough into each, taking care that each round meets the top of the cup. Bake unfilled for 5–10 minutes or until they begin to brown. Remove from oven.

Using a tablespoon, carefully fill each cup with cheese mixture, top with 2 or 3 tomato slices, and brush with olive oil. Sprinkle tartlets with ¼ cup (60 mL) cheese.

Bake on middle oven rack for 20–25 minutes or until pastry has browned and filling has set. Remove from oven and allow to cool on a baking rack for at least 15 minutes. Using a butter knife, gently pry each tartlet out.

Serve warm or at room temperature.

Makes 24 tartlets.

LYNN'S PIE CRUST

This is the pie crust that Amy's mom, Lynn, has made since forever. It's really easy to work with and yields generous portions so you can make a thick crust. And this crust is awesomely flaky because it's made with butter.

In a food processor, combine 1 ½ cups (375 mL) flour, salt, and sugar and pulse 4 times. Add butter and pulse 15–20 times, until mixture resembles cottage cheese and no dry flour is visible. Using a wooden spoon, redistribute dough in food processor.

Add remaining flour and process 6–8 times, then empty mixture into a medium bowl. Sprinkle with icy cold water and vodka. On a floured surface, using your hands, mix dough with a folding motion and divide into 2 even pieces. Cover and refrigerate for at least 30 minutes before rolling out on a floured surface.

Makes 2 9-in (23-cm) pie crusts or 24 tartlets.

INGREDIENTS

1 ½ (375 mL) cups whole milk ricotta

1 cup (250 mL) grated Parmesan or Pecorino Romano cheese (¾ cup [175 mL] for filling, ¼ cup [60 mL] for topping)

2 eggs

¼ cup (60 mL) chopped fresh basil

1 tsp salt

¼ tsp freshly ground black pepper

2 tbsp softened butter for muffin tin

2 9-in (23-cm) pie crusts, (recipe below) at room temperature and cut into 2.5-in (6.35-cm) rounds

1 lb (500 g) heirloom cherry tomatoes, cut into 3 or 4 rounds

2 tsp olive oil

Lynn's Pie Crust

2 ½ cups (625 mL) all-purpose flour

1 tsp salt

2 tbsp sugar (omit for savory crusts)

1 ¼ cups (310 mL) cold unsalted butter, cut into ¼-in (6-mm) slices

¼ cup (60 mL) iced water, strained

¼ cup (60 mL) cold vodka

EQUALITY FARMS IN BUFFALO, MINNESOTA, GROWS
COOL VARIETIES OF ORGANIC CHERRY HEIRLOOMS.
THEY ALSO OFFER JOB TRAINING AND EMPLOYMENT
FOR ADULTS WITH DEVELOPMENTAL DISABILITIES.

THREE SUMMER BRUSCHETTAS

A trio of warm-weather favorites for mid-summer gatherings. Pick up a few baguettes, make your own crostini (recipe below), and prepare all three. Or choose one that matches your palate and party theme. While these three complement each other nicely, each stands alone as a solo performer.

CROSTINI

Preheat oven to 350°F (180°C).

Cut baguette into ½-in (1-cm) slices and place on a baking sheet. Using a basting brush, brush olive oil over top of each slice and sprinkle each with salt.

Bake on middle oven rack for 10 minutes. Raise rack and switch oven function to broil.

Broil toasts for 1 minute, until lightly crisped on top. Cool slightly, then rub each slice with cut sides of garlic clove.

SUMMER SQUASH & RICOTTA BRUSCHETTA

In a large frying pan on high, heat olive oil. Add yellow squash, zucchini, onions, salt, and pepper. Sauté for 4 minutes, allowing squashes to lightly brown. Add garlic and sauté for 4–5 minutes, until squash is tender but not mushy. Remove from heat, stir in basil and capers, and allow to cool slightly. Stir in vinegar and ¼ cup (60ml) cheese.

To serve, spread about 1 tbsp ricotta atop each crostini and top with a scant 1 tbsp of squash mixture. Garnish with grated Pecorino Romano and more basil.

Makes about 24 bruschetta.

INGREDIENTS

Crostini
1 baguette
2 tbsp olive oil
1 tsp kosher salt
1 garlic clove, peeled and cut in half

Summer Squash & Ricotta Bruschetta
3 tbsp olive oil
1 small yellow squash, halved lengthwise and cut into ½-in (1-cm) wedges
1 small zucchini, halved lengthwise and cut into ½-in (1-cm) wedges
½ cup (125 mL) diced sweet onions
1 tsp kosher salt
½ tsp freshly ground black pepper
2 garlic cloves, peeled and minced
¼ cup (60 mL) fresh basil chiffonade
1 tbsp capers
1 tbsp white balsamic vinegar
¼ cup (60 mL) grated Pecorino Romano cheese
1 ½ cup (375 mL) whole milk ricotta
grated Pecorino Romano cheese, for garnish
fresh basil chiffonade, for garnish

GRILLED EGGPLANT BRUSCHETTA

Preheat oven to 350°F (180°C).

In a medium bowl, toss eggplant, tomatoes, and garlic in olive oil, salt, and pepper. Place vegetables on a parchment-lined baking sheet and bake for 35–40 minutes, tossing halfway through. Remove from oven, cool slightly, and place mixture in the bowl of a food processor. Sprinkle with fenugreek and pulse mixture 5 times. In a small bowl, combine lemon zest with yogurt and stir well.

To serve, spread 1 tbsp eggplant mixture on a crostini and garnish with ½ tbsp lemon yogurt. Sprinkle with chopped parsley.

Makes about 24 bruschetta.

SAFFRON-LEMON SHRIMP BRUSCHETTA

In a large frying pan on high heat, bring olive oil to a sizzle. Add shrimp, garlic, salt, pepper, and saffron, and sauté, tossing continuously, for 1 minute. Add wine and continue to cook until liquid reduces by half. Remove from heat and cool slightly. Stir in lemon juice and zest, green onions, and bell peppers. Top each crostini with two pieces of shrimp.

Makes about 24 bruschetta.

INGREDIENTS

Grilled Eggplant Bruschetta

1 large eggplant (about 1 lb [500 g]), cut in
   1-in (2.5-cm) cubes
½ lb (250 g) cherry tomatoes, halved
4 garlic cloves, halved
¼ cup (60 mL) olive oil
½ tsp kosher salt
¼ tsp freshly ground black pepper
¼ tsp ground fenugreek seeds
2 tsp freshly grated lemon zest
¾ cup (175 mL) plain Greek yogurt
3 tbsp chopped fresh parsley, for garnish

Saffron-Lemon Shrimp Bruschetta

2 tbsp olive oil
1 lb (500 g) medium raw shrimp, peeled
   and deveined, tails removed
2 garlic cloves, peeled and minced
1 tsp kosher salt
½ tsp freshly ground black pepper
¼ tsp saffron threads
¼ cup (60 mL) white wine
2 tsp freshly squeezed lemon juice
2 tsp lemon zest
4 green onions, green parts only, chopped
¼ cup (60 mL) finely diced red bell pepper

SWEET CORN RISOTTO WITH SHRIMP

Sweet local corn is one of the best things about summertime, and this brilliant risotto dish really lets its flavor shine! This small-portion format keeps it from being too "heavy," even on the hottest days.

Preheat oven to 450°F (230°C).

In a large saucepan on medium-high, bring stock to a low boil. Cover pan and reduce heat to low.

In a large frying pan on high, heat olive oil and butter until sizzling. Add onions and cook for 3 minutes, until translucent. Stir in rice, salt, and corn kernels. Cook for 3–4 minutes on medium-high heat, stirring occasionally, until rice is very lightly toasted. Stir in wine and cook until reduced by half, about 3 more minutes.

While continuously stirring, add warm chicken stock, about ⅓ cup (80 mL) at a time, allowing rice to absorb most of the existing liquid between additions, until it becomes creamy and is cooked through. Stir in Parmesan and lemon juice and zest until well incorporated, cover, and set aside, keeping warm.

In a large bowl, toss shrimp in olive oil, salt, and pepper. Place shrimp on baking sheet. Roast shrimp until just pink, firm, and cooked through, about 5–7 minutes. To grill shrimp, heat a charcoal or gas grill to about 350°F (180°C) and, using cooking spray, oil the grates. Toss shrimp in olive oil, salt, and pepper and lay flat on grill. Cook for 2 minutes on each side, until shrimp are grill-marked.

Portion equal amounts of risotto on small plates and top with shrimp, feta cheese, and basil. Serve warm.

Makes 12 servings.

INGREDIENTS

4 cups (1 L) chicken stock
2 tbsp olive oil
2 tbsp butter
1 cup (250 mL) chopped onions
1 ½ cups (375 mL) Arborio rice
1 ½ tsp salt
3 ears fresh sweet corn kernels, cut off cob
1 cup (250 mL) dry white wine
¾ cup (175 mL) grated Parmesan cheese
2 tbsp lemon juice
2 tsp lemon zest
24 medium raw shrimp, deveined, peeled, tail on
1 tbsp olive oil (for shrimp)
1 tsp salt
1 tsp freshly ground pepper
½ cup (125 mL) crumbled feta cheese
¼ cup (60 mL) fresh basil chiffonade, for garnish

GF

THIS IRRESISTIBLE SMALL PLATE IS SURE TO MOVE FAST AT ANY PARTY.

LAMB MEATBALLS WITH SPICED YOGURT CHUTNEY

We love the Middle Eastern flavors of this appetizer—earthy spices, cool yogurt, and pasture-fed lamb. Delicious any season, this appetizer pairs well with Marinated Chèvre with Honey, Rosemary & Marcona Almonds (p. 25), Chicken & Apricot Bastilla (p. 37), Roasted Cauliflower Pâté (p. 101), Mango Chicken Salad (p. 59), and Coconut Quinoa & Turmeric Ginger Apple Salad (p. 98).

LAMB MEATBALLS

Preheat oven to 300°F (150°C).

In a large frying pan on medium, heat 3 tbsp olive oil. Add onions and garlic and sauté, without browning, for about 4 minutes, until onions are translucent. In a large bowl, mix onions and garlic with lamb, rice, yogurt, eggs, cilantro, salt, pepper, cinnamon, cloves, and nutmeg until well blended. Using your hands, form mixture into balls, about 1 ½-in (4-cm) in diameter. Place meatballs on an ungreased baking sheet.

Reheat frying pan and add 3 tbsp olive oil. When hot, add meatballs, and working in small batches, cook, turning occasionally, for about 10 minutes or until lightly browned. Return cooked meatballs to baking sheet and bake for 7–8 minutes while preparing Spiced Yogurt Chutney.

Skewer each meatball with a toothpick and serve hot alongside yogurt chutney for dipping.

Makes about 40 meatballs.

SPICED YOGURT CHUTNEY

In a food processor, combine all ingredients and blend for 40 seconds. Scrape down sides and process another 15 seconds, until cilantro is entirely incorporated and sauce is smooth. Can be made ahead and refrigerated.

Makes 1 cup (250 mL) sauce.

INGREDIENTS

Lamb Meatballs
3 tbsp olive oil
1 ½ cups (375 mL) chopped onions
3 tbsp minced garlic
2 lb (900 g) ground lamb
¾ cup (175 mL) cooked white rice
¼ cup (60 mL) Greek yogurt
2 eggs, beaten
½ cup (125 mL) chopped fresh cilantro
2 tsp kosher salt
1 tsp freshly ground black pepper
¼ tsp ground cinnamon
⅛ tsp ground cloves
⅛ tsp ground nutmeg
3 tbsp olive oil

Spiced Yogurt Chutney
1 cup (250 mL) Greek yogurt
1 cup (250 mL) chopped fresh cilantro
½ tsp ground cumin
¼ tsp ground coriander
½ tsp ground fennel seeds
2 tbsp fresh lime juice
2 tsp white sugar

IF YOU DON'T CARE FOR LAMB, THE RECIPE WORKS PERFECTLY WELL WITH GROUND BEEF.

GF

PHOTOS BY ANDREW VICKERS

CARPACCIO & GREEN BEAN BUNDLES

Wherever she travels, Heidi loves to shop local for seasonal inspirations. This recipe came to fruition with a score of petite French *haricot vert* beans at the Santa Monica Farmers' Market, in California, followed by a trip to a neighborhood butcher shop, where she was seduced by a luscious cut of grass-fed beef tenderloin.

In a large pot, bring 5 qt (5 L) water to a boil.

Meanwhile, snip stem ends off green beans, but leave the sweet little curled tip on the other end. When water is at a rolling boil, add kosher salt and then green beans. Blanch for 5–7 minutes, until al dente. Drain beans and immediately douse with table salt while they are still hot, tossing to coat evenly. Set aside to cool.

Cut cheese into matchstick strips, ¼-in (6-mm) wide and 2–3-in (5–8 cm) long, and set aside.

Line a baking sheet with parchment and get ready to bundle! Stack together 4 or 5 green beans with a piece of cheese, wrap with a slice of raw tenderloin, and place on baking sheet. Keep chilled until serving.

After arranging bundles on a serving platter, sprinkle with olive oil, pink sea salt, and lemon zest. Squeeze lemon juice only on the meat (so it doesn't turn beans army green) and serve immediately.

Makes 24 bundles.

INGREDIENTS

1 lb (500 g) French green beans

2 tbsp kosher salt

1 tbsp table salt

¼-lb (125-g) wedge Pecorino Romano cheese

1 lb (500 g) grass-fed beef tenderloin, sliced paper-thin

2 tbsp extra virgin olive oil

1 tbsp freshly ground pink sea salt

1 lemon, zested and juiced

TO ENSURE PAPER-THIN SLICES OF BEEF, THE TENDERLOIN SHOULD BE FROZEN. PLACE YOUR ORDER A DAY IN ADVANCE AND REQUEST THAT THE BUTCHER FREEZE THE MEAT BEFORE SLICING. IF YOU HAVE A CRABBY BUTCHER, GIFTS OF FOOD PREPARED WITH THEIR MEAT ARE GUARANTEED TO WIN THEIR HEART.

GF

BABY HOT BROWNS

Created in Louisville, Kentucky's legendary Brown Hotel in the 1920s, the Hot Brown is an open-faced sandwich featuring turkey, Mornay sauce, tomatoes, and bacon, broiled until bubbly, and served with a knife and fork. Our version is handheld, eaten in 2 to 3 bites, and a Chowgirls' staff favorite.

Preheat oven to 350°F (180°C).

Lay baguette slices on a baking sheet and brush each with olive oil. Bake for about 10 minutes, until edges start to brown, then remove from oven, leaving oven at same temperature.

In a medium saucepan on medium heat, melt butter. Slowly add flour, whisking continuously, to create a smooth roux. Stir in milk, ¼ cup (60 mL) at a time, and continue to stir until sauce comes to a gentle boil. Remove from heat. Add Parmesan, salt, and pepper and stir until melted and well blended.

Top each baguette round with about a scant tablespoon of chopped turkey, then layer on sauce, tomato slice, and ½ tbsp cheddar. Bake for about 15 minutes, until set.

Immediately top appetizers with warm chopped bacon and serve hot.

Makes 30 servings.

INGREDIENTS

1 baguette, sliced into about 30 ½-in (1-cm) rounds
2 tbsp olive oil
3 tbsp butter
3 tbsp all-purpose flour
1 ½ cups (375 mL) milk
¼ cup (60 mL) freshly grated Parmesan cheese
¼ tsp salt
⅛ tsp freshly ground black pepper
½ lb (250 g) deli-style turkey breast, roughly chopped
4 Roma tomatoes, sliced
1 cup (250 mL) grated cheddar cheese
8 slices bacon, cooked and chopped

YOU CAN FIND AN ENTIRE KENTUCKY DERBY PARTY MENU RIGHT HERE IN THIS BOOK! BENEDICTINE FINGER SANDWICHES (P. 73), BABY HOT BROWNS (P. 71), CORN PUDDING (P. 58), BACON PECAN TARTLETS (P. 83), AND MINT JULEP SWEET TEA (P. 48).

BENEDICTINE FINGER SANDWICHES

Benedictine, a cool cucumber and cream cheese spread, is standard fare at any Southern spring gathering, particularly in Amy's home state of Kentucky. We serve it in finger sandwich form on raisin bread. This unlikely combination of flavors wins rave reviews every year at our Kentucky Derby party.

Peel and grate 1 cucumber. Place in a fine sieve over a small bowl. Using a paper towel, gently press out liquid. Discard pulp and place cucumber juice into a food processor. Add cream cheese, onions, mayonnaise, salt, and garlic granules. Process for 30 seconds until well blended.

Peel and thinly slice second cucumber and reserve for sandwich preparation.

To assemble sandwiches, spread a thin layer of cream cheese mixture on each slice of raisin bread. Add a single layer of cucumber slices to half the bread slices and top with remainder of bread slices, gently pressing them together. Using a sharp knife, remove crusts, then cut sandwiches diagonally into triangles. Serve immediately or refrigerate for up to 4 hours.

Makes 24 to 36 finger sandwiches.

INGREDIENTS

2 medium cucumbers
8 oz (230 g) cream cheese, softened
1 tbsp grated onions
1 tbsp mayonnaise
⅛ tsp salt
⅛ tsp garlic granules
1 16-oz (475-g) loaf thinly sliced raisin
    bread

SUMMER SHRUBS

Many people consider the shrub to be the oldest American cocktail; it made its debut during Colonial times. Vinegar was added to fruit as a preservative, allowing folks to enjoy summer's bounty year-round. Someone smart added booze, and voilà—the "shrub" was born! The fruit syrup bases of these cocktails will last for months when stored in the refrigerator.

BOURBON PEACH SHRUB

Amy's favorite fruit, the peach, has a short-lived season. Make sure you're only using flavorful, ripe ones, and your drinks will have not only real peach flavor, but a nice, rich color as well. It's fine to substitute a different variety of whiskey, but we think bourbon gives it a more genteel touch.

In a small saucepan on medium heat, dissolve sugar in water and bring to a boil. Add peaches and continue to boil, stirring occasionally, for 5–7 minutes, until peaches have dissolved. Remove from heat, stir in vinegar, and allow to cool completely. When cool, strain into a cocktail pitcher. Stir in bourbon and club soda.

Serve over ice in highball glasses, garnished with lime wedges.

Makes 10 cocktails.

RASPBERRY SHRUB

This recipe came to us by way of Chowgirl Jenny, a charming event planner and cocktail connoisseur, who created it as the signature drink for her June wedding. It became all the rage at our employee parties and debuted on our bar menu in the summer of 2014.

In a small saucepan on low heat, dissolve sugar in water and bring to a boil. Add raspberries and continue to boil, stirring occasionally, for 5–7 minutes, until raspberries have dissolved. Remove from heat, stir in vinegar, and allow to cool completely. When cool, strain into a cocktail pitcher. Stir in rum, ginger ale, and ginger beer. Serve over ice in highball glasses.

Makes 12 drinks.

INGREDIENTS

Bourbon Peach Shrub
½ cup (125 mL) sugar
½ cup (125 mL) water
3 ripe peaches, peeled and sliced
½ cup (125 mL) cider vinegar
3 cups (700 mL) bourbon
3 cups (700 mL) club soda
10 lime wedges, for serving

Raspberry Shrub
½ cup (125 mL) sugar
½ cup (125 mL) water
¾ cup (180 mL) fresh or frozen
   raspberries
6 oz (180 mL) white wine vinegar
3 cups (700 mL) dark Jamaican rum
3 cups (700 mL) ginger ale
3 cups (700 mL) ginger beer

THE BOURBON PEACH SHRUB IS
THE SOUTHERN BELLE OF OUR
COCKTAIL LIST.

WHITE SANGRIA

This refreshing summer punch also makes a great centerpiece for any bar or table. Colorful fruit peering through a stylish pitcher, beverage tureen, or punch bowl makes this cocktail particularly lovely and tempting. We call for peaches and raspberries, but feel free to experiment with whatever summer fruit looks best at the farmers' market that week. Careful ... it goes down fast!

In a large cocktail pitcher, beverage tureen, or punch bowl, combine wine, brandy, juice, and honey. Stir thoroughly to incorporate honey. Stir in peaches, raspberries, and mint. Serve over ice in highball glasses.

Makes 10 drinks.

INGREDIENTS

2 26-oz (750-mL) bottles Sauvignon Blanc
1 cup (250 mL) brandy
1 ½ cups (375 mL) pineapple juice
3 tbsp honey (preferably local), melted
2 ripe peaches, peeled and sliced
½ cup (125 mL) fresh raspberries
¼ cup (60 mL) fresh muddled mint

FOR an EVEN MORE FLAVORFUL SANGRIA,
MAKE THIS UP TO 24 HOURS IN ADVANCE.

SUMMER THYME

Come July, Midwesterners are cursing the major mess made on their sidewalks by mulberries. Heidi has found a way to turn that frown upside-down by making an amazing cocktail with this sweet fruit. If you don't have your own mulberry tree, certainly a friend or neighbor would be happy to spare a harvest.

COCKTAIL

In a large pitcher, combine liquors, syrup, and lemon juice. For each drink, pour ½ cup (125 mL) into a cocktail shaker with ice and shake for 8–10 seconds. Strain into a Cosmopolitan glass and top with 2 oz (60 mL) club soda or seltzer. Garnish with fresh thyme sprigs.

Makes 8 cocktails.

MULBERRY-THYME SYRUP

In a small saucepan on high, bring thyme and water to a boil. Reduce heat and allow to simmer for 15 minutes. Remove thyme and add mulberries. Bring to a boil again, then reduce heat and simmer for 30 minutes. Strain out mulberries through a fine mesh sieve to remove seeds, and return saucepan to low heat. Stir in sugar until thoroughly dissolved. Allow to cool.

Makes 1 cup (250 mL) syrup.

INGREDIENTS

Cocktail

16 oz (500 mL) vodka or gin
8 oz (250 mL) Chambord Liqueur
8 oz (250 mL) Mulberry Thyme Syrup
4 oz (120 mL) fresh lemon juice, strained
16 oz (500 mL) club soda or seltzer
8 fresh thyme sprigs, for garnish

Mulberry-Thyme Syrup

8 fresh thyme sprigs
1 ½ cups (375 mL) water
1 cup (250 mL) mulberries
1 cup (250 mL) sugar

BLACK RASPBERRIES MAKE A NICE SUBSTITUTE IF YOU HAVE A HARD TIME SOURCING MULBERRIES.

FALL

WHISKEY-GINGER COCKTAIL
MEATBALLS

BACON-PECAN TARTLETS

WILD MUSHROOM HOTDISH

THAI RED PEPPER SHOOTER

SMØRREBRØD, THREE WAYS

SWISS CHARD GRATIN

ANTIPASTO ROLLS

ROASTED FALL VEGETABLES
WITH SAFFRON AIOLI

ARANCINI WITH
SWEET TOMATO JAM

PROSCIUTTO-WRAPPED
PERSIMMONS

COCONUT QUINOA & TURMERIC
GINGER APPLE SALAD

VEGETABLE PÂTÉ TRIO

GRILLED SIRLOIN WITH FARRO
TOMATO SALAD

COLD SPICED CIDER

CORN-N-OIL

BANKRUPTCY ISLAND

FINOCCHIO FRIZZANTE

WHISKEY-GINGER COCKTAIL MEATBALLS

When Minneapolis food and beverage mogul Kieran Folliard launched his own brand of Irish whiskey, 2 Gingers, we hosted a private party in our gallery/dining space, Chowgirls Parlor. Amy created this irresistible sticky-sweet sauce of honey and citrus to pair with (guess what?) whiskey and ginger.

MEATBALLS

Preheat oven to 350°F (180°C).

In a large frying pan on high, heat olive and sesame oils. Add garlic, ginger, and shallots and sauté for 3 minutes until softened. Transfer to a medium bowl. Set pan aside.

Using your hands, combine ground beef and pork, salt, soy sauce, pepper, red pepper flakes, crumbs, egg, and orange zest in bowl with shallot mixture until all ingredients are well combined.

On a parchment-lined baking sheet, place 2 tbsp meatball mixture in mounds spaced 1 in (2.5 cm) apart. Using your hands, roll each mound into a ball.

SAUCE

Bake for 18–20 minutes or until cooked through.

Meanwhile, return frying pan to high heat. Add whiskey and orange juice and bring to a boil. When liquid is reduced to half, add butter and honey, and reduce heat to medium. Dissolve cornstarch in 2 tsp water and add to pan. Bring to a boil and stir until mixture thickens, about 3 minutes. Reduce heat to low, add lemon juice and meatballs to pan, and toss until well coated. Garnish with chopped green onions, sesame seeds, and orange zest and serve with cocktail toothpicks.

Makes about 24 meatballs.

SAMPLE A SHOT OF WHISKEY BEFORE YOU MAKE THIS RECIPE.
THEN USE YOUR SHOT GLASS AS A MEASURING CUP FOR THE
PERFECT SIZED MEATBALL!

INGREDIENTS

Meatballs
1 tbsp olive oil
2 tsp sesame oil
3 garlic cloves, minced
1 tbsp peeled and finely diced ginger
2 shallots, finely diced
1 lb (500 g) grass-fed ground beef
½ lb (250 g) ground pork
2 tsp kosher salt
2 tsp soy sauce
1 tsp freshly ground black pepper
¼ tsp red pepper flakes
1 cup (250 mL) rice cakes or crackers, processed to crumbs
1 egg
1 tbsp orange zest

Sauce
¼ cup (60 mL) bourbon or other aged whiskey
½ cup (125 mL) freshly squeezed orange juice
¼ cup (60 mL) salted butter
¼ cup (60 mL) honey (preferably local)
½ tsp cornstarch
1 tsp freshly squeezed lemon juice
2 green onions, chopped, for garnish
1 tbsp sesame seeds, for garnish
1 tbsp orange zest, for garnish

THESE MEATBALLS GO FAST! CONSIDER MAKING A DOUBLE BATCH IF YOU'RE GOING TO HAVE A LOT OF HUNGRY PEOPLE AT YOUR PARTY.

SWEET, SALTY, AND STICKY, BACON-PECAN TARTLETS ARE ONE OF OUR MOST DECADENT APPETIZERS.

BACON-PECAN TARTLETS

Bacon is everywhere these days, popping up not only in savory recipes but in cocktails, desserts, Internet memes, and even on socks and T-shirts! Keeping Chowgirls on trend, Amy tailored her mother's classic pecan pie recipe, adding maple syrup and bacon, of course, to create one of our most popular fall finger foods.

Preheat oven to 375°F (190°C).

In a medium saucepan on low heat, melt butter. Raise heat to medium and add maple syrup and sugar, whisking continuously, until sugar is dissolved and no longer grainy, about 8 minutes. Remove from heat and let cool for 15 minutes, stirring occasionally. Whisk in beaten eggs and vanilla until well combined. Set aside.

On a floured surface, roll out dough and cut into 2.5-in (6.35-cm) rounds. Butter each cup of a mini-muffin tin. Gently press in a round of pastry dough, making sure that each round meets the top of the cup. Add chopped bacon and chopped pecans to each cup, then fill with about 1 tbsp filling. Top each cup with a whole pecan.

Bake on middle oven rack for 20–25 minutes, until pastry has browned and filling set. Remove from oven and allow to cool on a baking rack for at least 15 minutes. Using a butter knife, gently pry each tartlet out of its cup. Serve warm or at room temperature.

Makes 24 pieces, or 32 if you're resourceful with re-rolling your dough scraps.

INGREDIENTS

½ cup (125 mL) butter
1 cup (250 mL) maple syrup
1 cup (250 mL) brown sugar
3 eggs, beaten
1 tsp vanilla extract
2 9-in (23-cm) pie crusts (recipe, p. 62)
1 tbsp butter, softened
1 lb (500 g) bacon, cooked crisp and
    chopped into small pieces
½ cup (250 mL) chopped pecans
32 whole pecans

THE RING LID FROM A REGULAR MOUTH MASON JAR IS A NICE SUBSTITUTE IF YOU DON'T HAVE A 2.5-IN (6.35-CM) PASTRY CUTTER.

WILD MUSHROOM HOTDISH

In our Midwest region, most folks call casserole "hotdish." Melding the flavors of three mushroom varieties, this rich and warming dip is a satisfying appetizer for the cool fall months. Serve hot with sliced baguette, crackers, or crostini for dipping.

Preheat oven to 350°F (180°C).

In a large frying pan on high heat, melt 1 tbsp butter with 1 tbsp olive oil. Working in small batches, add cremini mushrooms, salt, and pepper and sauté for 3–5 minutes, until soft. Remove mushrooms and set aside. Melt another tbsp butter and olive oil and, working in small batches, sauté portobello and shiitake mushrooms for about 5 minutes, until soft. Remove mushrooms and set aside.

Reduce heat to low and melt 1 tbsp butter. Whisk in flour to make a roux. When roux begins to brown, stir in milk and cream. On medium heat, bring to a boil. Add cheese and whisk until bubbling and thick. Stir in cooked mushrooms. Season to taste. Stir in truffle oil.

Transfer to a 2-qt (2-L) casserole dish or cast-iron frying pan. Sprinkle breadcrumbs over top and bake for 30–35 minutes, until heated through and breadcrumbs are browned.

Makes 4 cups (1 L) or about 30 servings.

INGREDIENTS

2 tbsp butter

2 tbsp olive oil

8-oz (230-g) cremini mushrooms, chopped

½ tsp salt

¼ tsp freshly ground black pepper

2 large portobello mushroom caps, thinly sliced

8-oz (230-g) shiitake, oyster, or other mushroom variety, sliced

1 tbsp butter

1 tbsp all-purpose flour

½ cup (125 mL) milk

½ cup (125 mL) heavy cream

½ cup (125 mL) grated pecorino or Parmesan cheese

salt and pepper, to taste

⅛ tsp truffle oil (optional)

¾ cup (175 mL) breadcrumbs tossed with 2 tbsp melted butter

THAI RED PEPPER SHOOTER

A former Chowgirls sous chef, Maren, brought this fantastic warming recipe to our table when "soup shots" were just beginning to bloom as a catering trend. With a slow, mellow burn at the finish, this intoxicating blend of red pepper, red curry, and coconut milk is a conversation-starting sip.

In a heavy-bottomed saucepan, heat coconut oil on medium-high heat. Add shallots and salt and sauté for 5–7 minutes, until very soft. Stir in red peppers, coconut milk, vinegar, and curry paste. Reduce heat to medium and stir until well combined. Remove from heat and allow to cool slightly.

In a blender on high speed, purée mixture in 3 batches, until smooth. Return purée to saucepan. Add vegetable broth a little at a time, until soup reaches desired consistency. Bring to a boil, then remove from heat. Using a glass measuring cup with a pour spout, pour into shot glasses. Top each glass with a sprinkling of cilantro and serve hot.

Makes 18 to 24 shots.

INGREDIENTS

1 tbsp coconut or olive oil
¼ cup (60 mL) diced shallots
½ tsp kosher salt
2 15-oz (430-g) jars roasted red peppers (not drained)
1 14-oz (398-mL) can coconut milk
1 tbsp rice wine vinegar
1–2 tbsp red curry paste, to taste
1 cup (250 mL) vegetable broth
¼ cup (60 mL) finely chopped fresh cilantro, for garnish

MAKE THIS SIMPLE SOUP UP TO 3 DAYS BEFORE YOUR PARTY. REHEAT JUST BEFORE SERVING.

SMØRREBRØD, THREE WAYS

Although neither Heidi nor Amy are of Swedish, Danish, or Norwegian descent, our world in Minnesota is known as "Little Scandinavia." We've become intrigued with that region's cuisine, and have adapted some recipes for catering. Adding smørrebrød, a classic Scandinavian open-faced sandwich snack, to our finger foods menu was a no-brainer.

HAM SALAD SMØRREBRØD

Preheat oven to 350°F (180°C).

On a large baking sheet, lay out bread slices. Brush with olive oil and sprinkle with salt. Bake for 10–15 minutes, until slightly crispy with darkened edges. Remove from oven and let cool.

In a food processor, pulse together garlic and green onions until minced. Add chopped ham and pulse 10–12 times, until finely chopped. Add mayonnaise, mustard, honey, Tabasco, and pepper. Process until smooth. Stir in chopped pickles.

To assemble, spread about 1 tbsp ham salad on each toast slice and top with apple slice and dill frond.

Makes about 24 portions.

...CONT'D P. 88

INGREDIENTS

½ loaf 16-oz (460-g) pumpernickel cocktail bread

2 tbsp olive oil

2 tsp kosher salt

1 garlic clove

3 small green onions, chopped

½ lb (250 g) deli-style smoked ham, chopped

⅓ cup (80 mL) mayonnaise

2 tsp stone-ground or Dijon mustard

1 tsp honey

2 dashes Tabasco sauce

¼ tsp freshly ground black pepper

2–3 small sweet pickles or cornichons, chopped

2 Honeycrisp (or McIntosh or Gala) apples, cored, halved lengthwise, and thinly sliced, for garnish

1 bunch fresh dill, torn into small fronds, for garnish

THIS RECIPE CAN EASILY BE DOUBLED FOR a LARGER CROWD.

MAKE ALL THREE SMØRREBRØD FOR AN IMPRESSIVE SPREAD.

AHI-AVOCADO SMØRREBRØD

Preheat oven to 350°F (180°C).

On a large baking sheet, lay out bread slices in a single layer and bake for 10 minutes. Remove from oven and flip each slice. Return to oven and continue to bake for 5–6 minutes, until crisp. Remove from oven and cool on a baking rack.

In a small bowl, mash avocadoes, using a fork, until smooth with very few lumps.

In a separate small bowl, whisk together orange and lime juice, ponzu, lime zest, garlic, and ginger. Continue to whisk while drizzling in sesame and avocado oils. When dressing has thickened, set aside.

In a medium frying pan on high, heat olive oil until almost smoking. Reduce heat slightly and add tuna steaks, searing for 2 minutes on each side until lightly crisped but raw in the center. Allow tuna to rest for 5 minutes. Using a sharp knife, thinly slice tuna into 32 evenly sized pieces. Set aside.

To assemble, top each toast with about 1 tbsp avocado, a slice of tuna, and a drizzle of dressing. Garnish with black and white sesame seeds, sunflower seeds, and watercress.

Makes 32 portions.

INGREDIENTS

8 slices dense multigrain bread, crusts removed, cut into four 2 x 3-in (5 x 8-cm) rectangles
3 ripe Hass avocadoes, peeled and pitted
2 tbsp freshly squeezed orange juice
1 tbsp freshly squeezed lime juice
2 tsp ponzu sauce
1 tsp finely grated lime zest
½ tsp finely minced garlic
1 tsp finely minced ginger
1 tbsp sesame oil
⅓ cup (80 mL) avocado oil
2 tbsp olive oil
3 sushi-grade ahi tuna steaks
1 ½ tbsp black sesame seeds
1 ½ tbsp white sesame seeds
3 tbsp shelled sunflower seeds
about ¼ cup (60 mL) watercress or microgreens, for garnish

SALMON-DILL SMØRREBRØD

Preheat oven to 350°F (180°C).

On a large baking sheet, lay out baguette slices in a single layer. Using a basting brush, liberally apply olive oil to each slice. Bake for 10 minutes. Remove from oven and flip each slice. Return to oven and continue to bake for 5–6 minutes, until crisp. Remove from oven and cool on a baking rack.

Pat salmon dry, salt and pepper both sides, and place on a baking sheet. Bake in center of oven for 20–25 minutes until translucent only in the center. Remove from oven and let cool.

Place cooked salmon in bowl of a stand mixer. Add cream cheese, garlic, lemon juice and zest, dill, and Tabasco, and mix on high speed until smooth.

Spread a generous dollop of salmon spread on each toast. Top with a slice of boiled egg, sliced radish, and a sprinkle of chopped watercress.

Makes about 30 portions.

INGREDIENTS

1 baguette, cut into 30 slices
3 tbsp olive oil
1 lb (500 g) boneless, skinless salmon filet
½ tsp kosher salt
¼ tsp freshly ground black pepper
16 oz (460 g) cream cheese, softened
2 tsp minced fresh garlic
3 tbsp freshly squeezed lemon juice
2 tsp lemon zest
2 tbsp chopped fresh dill
1 tsp Tabasco or other hot sauce
3 boiled eggs, sliced in ¼-in (6mm) thick rounds
4–6 red radishes, sliced thinly
3 tbsp chopped watercress or parsley, for garnish

SWISS CHARD GRATIN

One of our most popular dips as the chill of fall sets in, this gratin is slightly spicy and very hearty. Feel free to swap out the chard for other greens like kale, collards, or mustards—whatever is looking best at your local farmers' market. For even deeper flavor, use a smoked cheese instead of Gouda. Serve warm with crostini, crackers, or crudités.

Preheat oven to 350°F (180°C).

In a large frying pan on medium-high heat, melt olive oil and butter. When sizzling, add shallots, garlic, and jalapeño, and sauté for 2–3 minutes, being careful not to brown the garlic. Stir in chopped chard, salt, and pepper and raise heat to high. Sauté, tossing continuously, 1–2 minutes, until chard is partially wilted. Remove from heat, drain off excess liquid, and set aside.

In the bowl of a stand mixer with a paddle attachment, combine cream cheese, mayonnaise, milk, garlic powder, and nutmeg. Mix on medium speed for about 30 seconds, until smooth. Stir in cheese and cooked chard.

Pour mixture into a 1-qt (1-L) casserole dish or medium cast-iron frying pan. In a small bowl, toss breadcrumbs with salt, pepper, and melted butter until lightly coated. Top chard mixture with breadcrumbs and bake, uncovered, for 30–35 minutes, until sides are bubbling and crumbs are toasted.

Makes 3 cups (750 mL) or 24 servings.

INGREDIENTS

1 tbsp olive oil
1 tbsp butter
1 large shallot, peeled and diced
3 garlic cloves, minced
½ jalapeño pepper, seeded and diced
1 bunch Swiss chard (about 4 cups [1 L]), stems removed, roughly chopped
½ tsp kosher salt
¼ tsp freshly ground black pepper
8 oz (230 g) cream cheese, softened
2/3 cup (160 mL) mayonnaise
½ cup (125 mL) milk
½ tsp garlic powder
½ tsp freshly ground nutmeg
1 cup (250 mL) grated Gouda cheese
⅓ cup (80 mL) fresh breadcrumbs
salt and pepper, to taste (for breadcrumb topping)
1 tbsp melted butter (for breadcrumb topping)

THIS DISH WAS INSPIRED BY ONE OF OUR FAVORITE MIDWESTERN CHEESES, MARIEKE GOUDA, HANDCRAFTED BY A DUTCH FAMILY IN THE SMALL TOWN OF THORP, WISCONSIN.

ANTIPASTO ROLLS

When we started our business in 2004, we each came equipped with an arsenal of our own recipes from home entertaining. One of Heidi's proven winners, inspired by the antipasto creations of her friend Mia's Italian father, Ralph, was this pretty, hand-assembled cone of cured meats, cheese, and vegetables. To serve, stack on a platter and garnish with olives and fresh Italian parsley sprigs.

Drain artichoke hearts and slice each quarter into three smaller wedges. Place in a medium bowl. Drain roasted red peppers and slice into strips ¼-in (6-mm) wide and 2–3 in (5–8-cm) long. Place in a separate medium bowl. Slice cheese into matchstick strips, ¼-in (6-mm) wide and 2–3-in (5–8-cm) long. Place in a third medium bowl.

Cut prosciutto into 3-in (8-cm) squares. Keep refrigerated until ready to assemble rolls (warm prosciutto is prone to tearing.)

Line work surface with parchment or wax paper. Place meat and 3 bowls to your right. Place 8–10 slices of pepperoni in 2 rows on parchment, with about 3 in (8 cm) space between each slice. Place a slice of prosciutto half over each pepperoni, leaving left half of pepperoni exposed. Place a slice of cheese on the seam between each pepperoni and prosciutto pair. Top with a wedge of artichoke heart and, finally, a red pepper strip.

Once stacks are prepared, begin to roll. Start from the left and roll pepperoni over filling, pulling it tight and twisting bottom edge closed to create a cone shape. Continue to roll, and use prosciutto to seal bundle. Stack rolls in an airtight container, separating each layer with wax paper or parchment.

May be refrigerated overnight.

Makes 24 rolls.

INGREDIENTS

14-oz (398-mL) can quartered artichoke hearts, rinsed

7-oz (198-mL) jar roasted red peppers

¼-lb (125 g) wedge Pecorino Romano cheese

24 pieces, about ⅓ lb (170 g), thinly sliced prosciutto

24 pieces, about ¼ lb (125 g), thinly sliced 3-in (8-cm) sandwich-style pepperoni

ASK THE NiCE FOLKS aT YOUR NEiGHBORHOOD DELi TO MAKE YOUR LiFE EaSiER BY LaYERiNG WaX PaPER BETWEEN THE PROSCiUTTO SLiCES.

ROASTED FALL VEGETABLES WITH SAFFRON AIOLI

By far the most popular Chowgirls menu item is our roasted veg platter. An ideal side dish for any dinner entrée, it also makes an impressive presentation on an appetizer buffet. This straightforward preparation reveals the natural character of each vegetable. Simply delicious.

ROASTED FALL VEGETABLES

Preheat oven to 375°F (190°C).

In a large bowl, toss each vegetable separately in 2 tbsp olive oil. Add 1 tbsp salt and 1 tsp pepper to each vegetable, tossing again to ensure even distribution.

Place on parchment-lined baking sheets and roast each vegetable until soft enough to pierce with a fork and edges are golden, about 30 minutes. Softer vegetables such as bell peppers will take less time.

Display vegetables on a large platter and serve at room temperature with Saffron Aioli.

Makes 12 servings. (VV)

SAFFRON AIOLI

In a very small saucepan on low heat, combine vinegar and garlic and bring to a simmer or heat in a microwave for 30-60 seconds. Add saffron and stir to release its red tint. Add honey, stir until dissolved, and remove from heat. Set aside to cool for 10 minutes. Add mayonnaise, whisking until thoroughly combined.

Makes 1 cup (250 mL).

INGREDIENTS

Roasted Fall Vegetables

½ head cauliflower, stem removed and cut into florets

1 acorn or carnival squash, seeded and sliced into ½-in (1-cm) strips

2 red bell peppers, seeded and sliced into ½-in (1-cm) strips

½ head broccoli, stem removed and cut into florets

1 bunch slender carrots, peeled

⅔ cup (160 mL) olive oil

5 tbsp (75 mL) kosher salt

5 tsp freshly ground pepper

Saffron Aioli

3 tbsp red wine vinegar

2 garlic cloves, finely minced

1 pinch saffron thread, crumbled

1 tbsp honey

1 cup (250 mL) mayonnaise

YOU CAN MAKE ROASTED VEGGIES YEAR-ROUND, USING WHATEVER IS IN SEASON.

THIS SICILIAN STREET FOOD OF FILLED RISOTTO BALLS IS STARTING TO POP UP AT MORE AND MORE RESTAURANTS THESE DAYS. NOW YOU CAN MAKE YOUR OWN AT HOME.

ARANCINI WITH SWEET TOMATO JAM

Arancini means "little orange" in Italian, referring to the shape and size of this enticing appetizer, which is a popular street food in Sicily. Heidi learned the recipe on a cooking trip abroad and adapted it to Chowgirls' style by filling it with fresh mozzarella and pairing it with our Sweet Tomato Jam.

ARANCINI

In a large frying pan on medium heat, melt butter and olive oil. Sauté onions until soft, about 3 minutes. Add rice and sauté for 2 minutes, stirring until rice is evenly coated in oil. As rice begins to toast, add white wine, stirring while it dramatically sizzles and steams. Stir in saffron, garlic, salt, and pepper and sauté 2 minutes. Add broth and bring to a boil. Stir, cover, reduce heat to low, and simmer for 30 minutes. Remove from heat and stir in Parmesan. Transfer to a parchment-lined baking sheet, spreading risotto out evenly to cool.

Once cooled, in the palm of your hand, stack 1 tbsp risotto, 1 piece of mozzarella, and another 1 tbsp risotto. Roll in your hands to form a 2-in (5-cm) ball, then roll each ball in breadcrumbs and place on a baking sheet.

In a heavy frying pan on medium-high, heat olive oil. When oil is hot, pan fry arancini, 4 or 6 at a time, for about 5 minutes, turning to brown and crisp evenly.

Serve warm with a helping of Sweet Tomato Jam.

Makes 32 pieces.

SWEET TOMATO JAM

Preheat oven to 350°F (180°C).

In a medium bowl, toss cherry tomatoes with 1 tbsp olive oil to evenly coat. Add salt and pepper and toss again. On a parchment-lined baking sheet, spread tomatoes in a single layer. Roast for 20 minutes, until skins burst.

Transfer roasted tomatoes to a small saucepan. Add vinegar, 1 tbsp olive oil, and brown sugar. Bring to a boil over medium heat, stirring until sugar dissolves. Reduce heat, add remainder of ingredients, and simmer on low for 15 minutes, until shiny and glazed.

Makes 2 cups (500 mL).

INGREDIENTS

Arancini

1 tbsp butter

2 tbsp olive oil

1 small onion, diced

2 cups (500 mL) uncooked Arborio rice

1 cup (250 mL) white wine

2 pinches saffron threads

2 garlic cloves, minced

1 tsp salt

1 tsp freshly ground black pepper

4 cups (1 L) vegetable broth

½ cup (125 mL) grated Parmesan cheese

8 pieces ciliegine (cherry-sized balls) fresh mozzarella, cut into quarters

2 cups (500 mL) breadcrumbs

2 cups (500 mL) olive oil

Sweet Tomato Jam

1 pint (500 mL) cherry tomatoes

1 tbsp olive oil

1 tsp salt

1 tsp freshly ground black pepper

½ cup (125 mL) red wine vinegar

1 tbsp olive oil

¼ cup (60 mL) brown sugar

¼ tsp ground cayenne pepper

¼ tsp ground cloves

½ tsp ground cumin

½ tsp ground cinnamon

1 garlic clove, minced

1 tsp peeled, minced fresh ginger

PROSCIUTTO-WRAPPED PERSIMMONS

If you're lucky enough to live in an area where the gorgeous persimmon grows locally, behold your autumnal blessings. This quick and easy appetizer uses the squat, flat-bottomed Fuyu persimmons, which are most enjoyable when crisp and firm. Their subtle floral flavor contrasts with the saltiness of cured meat and is finished with refreshing mint.

Hull the stems and leaves from persimmons. Cut each in half vertically, then cut each half into vertical thirds, removing black seeds as necessary. Cut prosciutto pieces in half lengthwise or tear apart if there is a natural separation in the meat. Wrap prosciutto pieces around persimmon slices ending on cut side of fruit. Position mint leaf where prosciutto wrap ends and skewer with a toothpick.

Makes 24 pieces.

INGREDIENTS

4 Fuyu persimmons
12 slices prosciutto
24 mint leaves

HEIDI HIGHLY RECOMMENDS a NOVEMBER PERSIMMON PILGRIMAGE TO CALIFORNIA, WHERE AT MOST FARMERS' MARKETS, YOU CAN GET TO KNOW THIS DIVINE FRUIT IN ITS MYRIAD OF SHAPES AND TEXTURES.

EVER WONDERED WHAT TO MAKE WITH THE BRIGHT, BEAUTIFUL, EXOTIC PERSIMMON? THIS RECIPE IS THE ANSWER!

COCONUT QUINOA & TURMERIC GINGER APPLE SALAD

Heidi created this small plate for the launch of The Plant Provocateur, an exotic floral boutique in Los Angeles. Colored by turmeric and flavored by ginger, the recipe originally featured crisp fresh Korean dates, a.k.a. jujubes, found at the Santa Monica Farmers' Market. Here we adapted it with a more commonplace fall fruit, the simple apple.

QUINOA

In a medium saucepan, mix together all ingredients. Bring to a boil on high heat, stir, and cover. Reduce heat to low and simmer for 15 minutes. While quinoa cooks, prepare rest of salad.

TURMERIC GINGER APPLES

Cut apples into ¼-in (6-mm) slices, then cut again into thirds to make triangle-shaped wedges. In a frying pan on high, heat olive oil. Reduce heat to medium, add apple pieces, and cook for 1 minute. Add ginger and turmeric, and cook for another minute, keeping apples crisp.

For each small plate, portion out 2 tbsp quinoa, top with 1 tsp sliced almonds, 1 tbsp turmeric ginger apples, and a few pomegranate seeds.

Makes 16 small plates.

INGREDIENTS

Quinoa
1 cup (250 mL) rainbow quinoa
2 cups (500 mL) coconut milk
3 cinnamon sticks
16 pitted dates, sliced into thin rounds

Turmeric Ginger Apples
2 Honeycrisp (or McIntosh or Gala) apples
2 tbsp olive oil
1-in (2.5-cm) piece ginger, peeled and grated
1-in (2.5-cm) piece turmeric root, peeled and grated
1 cup (250 mL) sliced almonds, for garnish
½ cup (125 mL) pomegranate seeds, for garnish

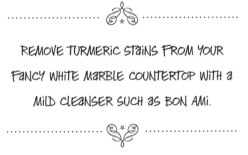

REMOVE TURMERIC STAINS FROM YOUR FANCY WHITE MARBLE COUNTERTOP WITH A MILD CLEANSER SUCH AS BON AMI.

THIS SMALL PLATE IS A
GREAT OFFERING FOR YOUR
HEALTH-CONSCIOUS FRIENDS.

VEGETABLE PÂTÉ TRIO

These vegetable pâtés are all terrific on their own, but we often serve them as a trio for a fun vegetarian option at parties. The flavors complement each other nicely, and all of them can be made vegan by substituting margarine or olive oil for the butter.

MUSHROOM-PECAN PÂTÉ

In a small bowl, soak pecans in cold water for at least 1 hour.

In a large, heavy-bottomed frying pan on medium heat, sauté shallots and garlic in olive oil for about 4 minutes. Increase heat to high and add mushrooms a handful at a time, stirring continuously. Continue to cook over high heat for 5 to 7 minutes, until mushrooms are soft. Add wine and continue to cook for 2–3 minutes, until liquids have reduced by half. Reduce heat to low and add butter, salt, pepper, and 2 tsp thyme, stirring until butter has just melted. Set aside and allow to cool slightly. Pick a few of the prettiest mushrooms and reserve for garnish.

Drain pecans and transfer to a food processor. Add mushroom mixture and lemon juice and purée for about 45 seconds, until very smooth.

Transfer mixture to a small bowl lined with plastic wrap. Smooth top of mixture, cover, and chill for at least 3 hours. When ready to serve, invert bowl on to a serving plate, remove plastic wrap, and garnish molded pâté with fresh thyme and reserved mushrooms.

Makes 1 cup (500 mL). (DF) (GF) (V)

EDAMAME PÂTÉ

Preheat oven to 350°F (180°C).

Rinse and drain edamame and transfer to a small bowl. Add 1 tbsp sesame oil, the salt and pepper, and toss thoroughly. Transfer to a parchment-lined baking sheet and roast for 15 minutes, until edges are barely golden. Remove from oven and let cool.

Use a paring knife to remove a ribbon of orange peel and reserve for garnish. Extract juice from orange and transfer to a food processor. Add green onions and process on high speed until well blended.

Add roasted edamame, chili powder, and 2 tbsp sesame oil to food

INGREDIENTS

Mushroom-Pecan Pâté
¾ cup (175 mL) pecan halves

1 shallot, roughly chopped

3 garlic cloves, roughly chopped

3 tbsp olive oil

8 oz (230 g) cremini or portobello mushrooms, sliced

4 oz (115 g) shiitake or other wild mushrooms, sliced

¼ cup (60 mL) white wine

3 tbsp unsalted butter

1 ½ tsp kosher salt

1 tsp freshly ground black pepper

2 tsp chopped fresh thyme, plus more for garnish

2 tsp freshly squeezed lemon juice

Edamame Pâté
10 oz (300 g) frozen shelled organic edamame (soybeans), thawed

1 tbsp sesame oil

1 tsp salt

1 tsp freshly ground black pepper

1 orange (peel on, for garnish)

4 green onions, green parts only, roughly chopped

2 tsp chili powder

2 tbsp sesame oil

black sesame seeds, for garnish

(GF) (V)

processor and process on high until smooth. Place mixture in a small bowl lined with plastic wrap. Smooth top of mixture, cover with plastic wrap, and refrigerate for at least 4 hours, up to 3 days. When ready to serve, keep very cold and invert bowl onto a small plate or platter, releasing pâté. Remove plastic and garnish with sesame seeds and curled orange peel.

Makes 2 cups (500 mL). (DF) (GF) (VV)

ROASTED CAULIFLOWER PÂTÉ

Preheat oven to 350°F (180°C).

In a pot fitted with a steamer on medium heat, steam cauliflower for 10 minutes, until softened. Transfer to a large bowl. Drizzle with coconut oil and sprinkle with salt and pepper. On a parchment-lined sheet pan, lay cauliflower in a single layer. Bake for 35–40 minutes, tossing occasionally, until cauliflower is browned. Set aside a roasted floret or two for a flavor-cue garnish.

Meanwhile, on medium heat, melt butter in a medium frying pan. Add onions and sauté, stirring occasionally for 8–10 minutes, until softened and lightly caramelized.

In a food processor, combine roasted cauliflower and onions and sprinkle with garam masala. Process until smooth.

Transfer mixture to a small bowl lined with plastic wrap. Smooth top of mixture, cover, and chill for at least 3 hours. When ready to serve, invert bowl onto a serving plate, remove plastic wrap, and garnish molded pâté with fresh parsley and reserved roasted cauliflower florets.

Makes 1 cup (250 mL). (DF) (GF) (V)

INGREDIENTS

Roasted Cauliflower Pâté

2 cups (500 mL) cauliflower florets
¼ cup (60 mL) coconut oil, melted
1 ½ tsp kosher salt
½ tsp freshly ground black pepper
3 tbsp butter
1 small yellow onion, chopped
2 tsp garam masala
2 tsp chopped fresh parsley, for garnish

GRILLED SIRLOIN WITH FARRO TOMATO SALAD

Farro is one of our favorite on-trend ancient grains. Packed with protein, its hearty texture makes it ideal to pair with steak. Roasting the tomatoes for the salad adds a really great tang. We prefer the sirloin cooked medium-rare, but you can add or subtract time on the grill if you and your guests have other ideas.

Preheat oven to 350°F (180°C).

In a small bowl, combine salt, pepper, garlic powder, tarragon, and cayenne to create a dry rub for the steak. Pat steak dry with a paper towel, then coat with herb and spice mixture. Set aside, allowing it to come to room temperature.

Rinse farro in a fine-mesh sieve. In a medium pot on high heat, combine farro with stock and bring to a boil. Stir and reduce heat to low. Cover and simmer for 20 minutes, until tender.

While farro cooks, halve cherry tomatoes and place them, seed side up, on a parchment-lined baking sheet. Using a basting brush, brush liberally with olive oil and sprinkle with kosher salt. Roast for 30 minutes, until slightly browned and softened.

In a large frying pan over high heat, heat 2 tbsp olive oil. Add garlic and spinach and sauté, stirring continuously, for 1–2 minutes or until about half the spinach is soft and wilted. Season with salt and pepper. Remove from heat and let cool.

In a large bowl, combine cooked farro, roasted tomatoes, and spinach-garlic mixture, tossing until well combined. Stir in feta and mint and season to taste with salt and pepper.

Heat a gas or charcoal grill to 350° (180°C). If using a broiler, preheat to 525°F (275°C) and preheat a cast-iron frying pan. Grill steak, covered, for 6–7 minutes, then turn and cook for another 6–7 minutes for medium-rare. If broiling, place steak in preheated frying pan and place 2–3 in (5–8 cm) from flame. Broil for about 4 minutes per side. Set aside and allow to rest at least 15 minutes before slicing. Slice thinly on the diagonal and set aside.

To serve: Spoon about ¼ cup (60 mL) salad onto each appetizer plate and place 1–2 strips steak alongside. Garnish with fresh mint leaves.

Makes 16 impressive small plates.

INGREDIENTS

1 tbsp kosher salt
1 tbsp freshly ground black pepper
2 tsp garlic powder
1 tbsp dried tarragon
⅛ tsp cayenne pepper
1 lb (500 g) sirloin, about
   1 ½-in (4-cm) thick

Salad

2 cups (500 mL) pearled farro
4 cups (1 L) chicken stock
1 lb (500 g) cherry tomatoes
2 tbsp olive oil
kosher salt, to taste
2 tbsp olive oil (for sautéing spinach)
2 garlic cloves, minced
4 cups (1 L) firmly packed baby spinach
salt and ground black pepper, to taste
½ cup (125 mL) chopped or crumbled feta
   cheese
¼ cup (60 mL) chopped fresh mint
salt and pepper, to taste
fresh mint leaves, for garnish

IF YOU NEED TO BUDGET YOUR TIME, MAKE THE ROASTED TOMATOES AHEAD OF TIME AND REFRIGERATE. BRING UP TO ROOM TEMP BEFORE ADDING TO SALAD.

WHAT WOULD MICHAEL POLLAN DO? USE GRASS-FED BEEF! IN THE MIDWEST, OUR ALLEGIANCE LIES WITH THOUSAND HILLS CATTLE COMPANY, A SOCIALLY AND ENVIRONMENTALLY CONSCIOUS BUSINESS THAT'S GROWN ALONGSIDE OURS FOR MORE THAN A DECADE.

THIS COCKTAIL IS A LOVELY BLEND OF HARD AND SWEET CIDERS WITH WHISKEY AND SPICES.

COLD SPICED CIDER

Born and raised in the Bluegrass State, Amy is always looking for new ways to serve Kentucky bourbon. This whiskey-spiked drink provides all the comforts of a hot-spiced cider in a cool rocks-style cocktail.

In a small saucepan on medium heat, combine apple cider, cinnamon, star anise, cloves, orange slices, and ginger and bring to a boil. Reduce heat and simmer for 30 minutes to make a concentrate. Set aside and let cool.

Combine mulled apple cider, bourbon, pear cider, and cold apple cider in a large cocktail pitcher. Stir well and pour over ice. Garnish with orange zest and star anise.

Makes 8 servings.

INGREDIENTS

2 cups (500 mL) apple cider (for mulling)

2 cinnamon sticks

6 star anise

1 tsp whole cloves

1 orange, sliced

2 in (5 cm) fresh ginger, peeled and sliced lengthwise

1 cup (250 mL) bourbon

2 12-oz (355-mL) bottles hard pear cider

2 cups (500 mL) cold apple cider (for finishing)

1 tbsp orange zest, for garnish

8 star anise, for garnish

CORN-N-OIL

There's little detail to be found on the origin of this cocktail and its name, but we can tell you it's totally dark. So dark it made Heidi have a flashback to when she, as a four-year-old root-beer connoisseur, mistakenly drank motor oil from an A&W mug in her dad's motorcycle shop. We assure you this concoction tastes much better and will not require a call to Poison Control.

Mix rum, Velvet Falernum, lime juice, and Angostura Bitters into a cocktail pitcher. Stir well. Serve over ice in highball glasses. Garnish with lime wedge.

Makes 8 cocktails.

INGREDIENTS

16 oz (500 mL) blackstrap rum

8 oz (250 mL) Velvet Falernum liqueur

6 oz 175 mL) lime juice

8 dashes Angostura Bitters

1 lime, cut into 8 wedges, for garnish

BANKRUPTCY ISLAND

Our shiny new bar manager, Onno, was kind enough to bring a Greek friend's family drink to our menu. Seemingly light with nutty and floral flavors, this unique wine spritzer packs a punch, so pace yourself!

COCKTAIL

Mix together all ingredients except seltzer. For each cocktail, pour 4 ¼ oz (125 mL) of the mix into a cocktail shaker with ice and shake for 8–10 seconds. Strain into a wine glass and top with 2 oz (60 mL) seltzer.

Makes 8 cocktails.

ORGEAT

Soak almonds in 2 ½ cups (625 mL) water for 30 minutes. Strain and transfer to a food processor. Pulse for 15 seconds. Transfer to a medium bowl and soak in 3 cups (700 mL) water for at least 6 hours or overnight. Strain out almonds and reserve water. Add brandy, orange blossom water, and sugar to almond water to create a simple syrup. Stir well to combine.

INGREDIENTS

Cocktail

16 oz (500 mL) Retsina (dry white wine made in Greece)

10 oz (310 mL) St. Germaine (elderflower liquor)

4 oz (125 mL) Orgeat (almond simple syrup, recipe below)

4 oz (125 mL) lime juice

16 oz (500 mL) club soda or seltzer

Orgeat

2 cups (500 mL) almonds

1 oz (30 mL) brandy

1 tsp orange blossom water

2 cups (500 mL) sugar

ORGEAT CAN ALSO BE PURCHASED AT LIQUOR OR SPECIALTY FOOD STORES.

FINOCCHIO FRIZZANTE

We love to mix fresh juice blends into our cocktails. When Amy hit upon the fabulous flavor combo of pear and fennel, we knew we had the essential elements for an elegant drink. Use D'Anjou pears for a dry character, Bartlett for a sweeter flavor, or a bushel from your neighbor's tree for the most honest taste of all.

In an electric juicer, juice fennel and pears together. Using a fine mesh sieve or cheesecloth, pour into a cocktail pitcher, straining solids. Add vodka, prosecco, and lemon juice and stir to combine well. Pour over ice into 8 highball glasses and garnish each glass with a sprig of fresh thyme.

Makes 8 cocktails.

INGREDIENTS

2 large fennel bulbs
3 D'Anjou or Bartlett pears
1 cup (250 mL) vodka
4 cups (1 L) prosecco
2 tbsp freshly squeezed lemon juice
8 fresh thyme sprigs, for garnish

IT'S BEST TO USE PEARS THAT ARE JUST ON THE CUSP OF RIPENESS; OVERRIPE FRUIT CAN CAUSE A PULPY JUICE EXPERIENCE.

THIS LIGHT AND REFRESHING COCKTAIL MAKES A DELICIOUS ADDITION TO A BRUNCH GATHERING.

PHOTOS BY CHOWGIRLS STAFF

WINTER

PLOUGHMAN'S PLATTER

MUSHROOM FRITTERS WITH
ROASTED TOMATO COULIS

ITALIAN BEEF SLIDERS

SWEDISH MEATBALLS

CRAB & GREEN CHILE GRATIN

TAPENADE TRIO

BECCA'S BUTTERNUT BISQUE

CORN PANCAKES WITH
CARNITAS & PICKLED RED ONION

IRON RANGE PASTIES

WINTER SQUASH & SAUSAGE
SKEWERS

LOCAL BEER FONDUE

BEETS & BURRATA

PORK TENDERLOIN WITH
CHERRY-ROSEMARY
MARMALADE

DUCK À L'ORANGE
FIRECRACKER ROLLS

CHOWGIRLS GLÖGG

SAGE WOODSTOCK

HOT ROD TODDY

POP'S EGGNOG

PLOUGHMAN'S PLATTER

A concept more than an actual recipe, this savory dish looks best served on a wooden board or pewter platter. Source bread, cured meats, cheeses, mushrooms, and root vegetables (roasting and pickling recipes below) from makers close to home and create a work of art that allows your guests to pick and choose the tastes they prefer. Here are some of our favorite elements of a Ploughman's Platter.

SWEET ONION JAM

In a large frying pan on high, heat olive oil. Stir in onions, fennel, salt, and pepper. Reduce heat to medium and cook for 10 minutes. Reduce heat to low and continue to cook, stirring occasionally, for 20 minutes, until onions and fennel have softened and lightly caramelized.

Meanwhile, in a small saucepan, cover golden raisins with 2 cups (500 mL) water and bring to a boil on high heat. Reduce heat to medium-low and simmer for 15 minutes, until raisins have softened. Drain well and add to onion-fennel mixture. Add 2 tbsp water. Cook on medium heat for an additional 5 minutes. Cool slightly.

In a food processor, add onion-fennel-raisin mixture. Pulse 12 times, until ingredients are well combined. Stir in vinegar and chopped thyme, and season to taste with salt and pepper.

Makes 1 cup (250 mL).

ROASTED MUSHROOMS

Preheat oven to 400°F (200°C).

In a medium bowl, toss mushrooms, olive oil, garlic, salt, and pepper. Line a baking sheet with parchment paper. Spread mushrooms in a single layer on sheet and bake for 30–40 minutes, tossing halfway through, until crisped at the edges. Garnish with thyme leaves, if using.

Makes ¾ cup (175 mL).

...CONT'D ON P. 114

INGREDIENTS

Sweet Onion Jam

¼ cup (60 mL) olive oil

2 yellow onions, cut in half and thinly sliced

1 fennel bulb, thinly sliced (white part only)

1 tsp kosher salt

½ tsp freshly ground black pepper

½ cup (125 mL) golden raisins

1 tsp white wine vinegar

2 tsp chopped fresh thyme leaves

kosher salt and ground black pepper, to taste

Roasted Mushrooms

1 lb (500 g) mixed mushrooms (oyster, shiitake, morels, cremini, etc.)

2 tbsp olive oil

2 garlic cloves, minced

1 tsp salt

freshly ground black pepper, to taste

½ tsp fresh thyme leaves (optional)

ANOTHER GREAT OPPORTUNITY TO SHOWCASE THE TALENTS OF OUR LOCAL FOOD SCENE. WE USE COPPA AND BIG CHET'S SALUMI FROM RED TABLE MEAT CO. IN NORTHEAST MINNEAPOLIS.

PICKLED VEGETABLES

In a medium saucepan, bring 2 cups (500 mL) water to a boil. Add garlic, and cook for 5 minutes. Add vinegar and salt, stirring until salt dissolves. Remove from heat.

Place cauliflower, carrots, sunchokes, curry, mustard seed, and peppercorns in a quart jar or other heat-proof container. Pour brine over vegetables to cover completely. Let cool, then cover and refrigerate for at least 3 hours or up to 4 weeks.

Makes 1 qt (1 L).

INGREDIENTS

Pickled Vegetables

5 garlic cloves, peeled
1 cup (250 mL) cider vinegar
3 tsp kosher salt
½ head cauliflower, cut into small florets
6 carrots, peeled and sliced
½ lb sunchokes (a.k.a. Jerusalem artichokes), sliced thinly
¼ tsp curry powder
1 tsp mustard seeds
1 tsp black peppercorns

MUSHROOM FRITTERS WITH ROASTED TOMATO COULIS

This small plate is one of our most popular vegetarian offerings brought to us by our stylist, the extraordinary Meg. We recommend using a variety of mushrooms; some of our favorites are cremini, oyster, and fresh shiitake.

MUSHROOM FRITTERS

In a large frying pan on medium, heat olive oil and butter until gently sizzling. Raise heat to medium-high and add shallots and mushrooms. Continue to cook for 7–10 minutes, until mushrooms are cooked through and have started to brown. Season with salt and pepper. Increase heat to high, then add sherry or vermouth, and boil it down until nearly completely reduced. Wrap mushroom mixture in a very clean kitchen towel and squeeze tightly to remove excess liquid. Transfer to a large bowl. Rinse frying pan and return to stovetop.

To mushroom mixture, add ½ cup (125 mL) breadcrumbs, cheeses, tarragon, and cream, and stir until combined. Using a ¼ cup (60 mL) measure, form mixture into balls. Flatten using your hands. Dredge each disc in flour, dip in beaten eggs, then coat with breadcrumbs.

In frying pan on medium heat, fry fritters in vegetable oil a few at a time, about 6 minutes per side, until brown and crispy. Remove from pan and drain on paper towels. Keep warm.

To serve, top each fritter with about 2 tbsp Tomato Coulis.

Makes 24 fritters.

TOMATO COULIS

In a blender or food processor, combine tomatoes, garlic, and olive oil and process until smooth. Add basil, salt, and pepper. Transfer to a small saucepan and bring to a boil. Let boil for 15 minutes, then remove from heat.

Makes 2 cups (500 mL).

INGREDIENTS

Mushroom Fritters

3 tbsp olive oil (for sautéing mushrooms)

2 tbsp unsalted butter

½ cup (125 mL) finely chopped shallots

1 lb (500 g) finely chopped fresh
   mushrooms

1 ½ tsp kosher salt

½ tsp freshly ground black pepper

½ cup (125 mL) dry sherry or vermouth

½ cup (125 mL) dry white breadcrumbs

½ cup (125 mL) grated pecorino or
   Parmesan cheese

½ cup (125 mL) grated Manchego cheese

¼ cup (60 mL) finely chopped fresh
   tarragon

¼ cup (60 mL) heavy cream

½ cup (125 mL) all-purpose flour

2 eggs, beaten

¾ cup (175 mL) dry white breadcrumbs

½ cup (125 mL) light vegetable oil

Tomato Coulis

1 14-oz can (398-mL) San Marzano or
   other imported whole tomatoes,
   drained

1 garlic clove

1 tbsp olive oil

3 tbsp chopped fresh basil, plus more for
   garnish

salt and ground black pepper, to taste

ITALIAN BEEF SLIDERS

A perennial favorite of Amy's family, this pulled-beef sandwich needs a lot of oven time but is totally worth it! Party guests will agree. Another cooking option? Use a slow cooker set to high for 6–7 hours. These sandwiches are easily enhanced by almost any cheese. We prefer Provolone.

Preheat oven to 350°F (180°C).

In a large Dutch oven on high, heat olive oil until sizzling. Season chuck roast with salt and pepper and add to pot, searing each side for about 3 minutes or until browned. Remove from heat and add garlic, beer, stock, tomatoes, red pepper flakes, basil, oregano, and bay leaves.

Cover pot and place in oven. Bake, turning roast occasionally, for 3 hours. Remove lid, stir in pepperoncini, return to oven uncovered, and cook for 1 hour.

Beef is ready when it can be easily pulled from the center outward using two forks. Shred beef in this fashion and stir to incorporate juices and peppers.

To serve: Slice slider buns and, using tongs, heap a generous portion of meat onto each. Can be served with its juice for dipping, if desired.

Makes 24 to 30 sandwiches.

INGREDIENTS

3 tbsp olive oil
3 lb (1.5 k) chuck roast
1 tbsp kosher salt
2 tsp freshly ground black pepper
6 garlic cloves, minced
1 12-oz (355-mL) can lager-style beer
1 qt (1 L) beef stock
1 14-oz (398-mL) can diced tomatoes
1–2 tsp red pepper flakes, to taste
2 tsp dried basil
1 tsp dried oregano
3 bay leaves
1 12-oz (355-mL) jar pepperoncini or
   banana pepper rings, with juice
24–30 slider buns

(DF)

SWEDISH MEATBALLS

Here in Minnesota, Swedish meatballs are a staple of church dinners and holiday meals and, when scaled down in size, as a cold-weather appetizer. Our recipe is a gift from our beloved first employee, Maari, straight from her Swedish grandma's recipe box. Everyone adores this Scandinavian classic!

In a large frying pan on medium-high, heat 1 tbsp olive oil and 1 tbsp butter until sizzling. Add onions and sauté for 5 minutes, until slightly translucent. Transfer onions to a bowl and let cool.

In a large bowl, using your hands, mix cooked onions with beef, pork, salt, egg, and breadcrumbs, until well combined. Form meatballs using a heaping tablespoon measure, smoothing them into balls with your hands, and set aside in a single layer.

Preheat oven to 325°F (160°C).

In a large frying pan on medium-high, heat 2 tbsp olive oil and 2 tbsp butter until almost smoking. Reduce heat to medium and add meatballs in batches. Cook, rotating occasionally, until browned, about 10 minutes. Reserve pan drippings. Transfer meatballs to a 9 x13-in (3.5-L) casserole dish. Bake for 15 minutes. Meanwhile, prepare the gravy.

Return frying pan with drippings to medium heat and add flour. Whisking continuously, brown flour for 2–3 minutes, taking care not to let it burn.

Add beef broth, 1 cup (250 mL) at a time, thickening mixture between each addition and whisking often, until a nice gravy develops. Add cream, heat through, and remove from burner.

Remove meatballs from oven, pour gravy over them, and toss gently to coat. Sprinkle with parsley, insert a toothpick in each, and serve hot.

Makes about 30 meatballs.

INGREDIENTS

1 tbsp olive oil
1 tbsp butter
1 small onion, diced
1 ½ lb (750 g) ground beef
1 ½ lb (750 g) ground pork
2 tsp salt
1 egg, beaten
¾ cup (175 mL) plain breadcrumbs
2 tbsp olive oil
2 tbsp butter
⅓ cup (80 mL) all-purpose flour
3 cups (700 mL) beef broth
1 cup (250 mL) heavy cream
3 tbsp fresh chopped parsley, for garnish

FOR A RUSTIC PRESENTATION, USE A CAST-IRON FRYING PAN FOR THIS DECADENT CRAB & GREEN CHILE GRATIN. BLUE CORN CHIPS OFFER NICE VISUAL CONTRAST.

CRAB & GREEN CHILE GRATIN

Our hot seafood dip has gotten rave reviews through the years. Worth the indulgence to warm up a winter party, it's a unique addition to any Mexican menu and goes great with margaritas! Serve hot with crostini or tortilla chips.

Preheat oven to 350°F (180°C).

In a medium frying pan on medium-high heat, melt butter. Add shallots and sauté until soft and transparent, about 3 minutes. Set pan aside.

In the bowl of a stand mixer using a paddle attachment, beat cream cheese until smooth. Add sour cream, half and half, cheese, lemon juice, and Worcestershire sauce and continue to mix until all ingredients are blended. Season with cayenne, Old Bay, dry mustard, salt, and pepper and stir to combine well.

Stir in sautéed shallots, crab, and green chiles and transfer to a lightly buttered baking dish. Reheat frying pan and melt 2 tbsp butter. Toss together breadcrumbs and paprika and mix in melted butter until evenly distributed. Sprinkle breadcrumbs over crab mixture.

Bake uncovered for 30–35 minutes, until browned at edges and bubbling. Remove from oven and sprinkle with parsley.

Makes about 25–30 servings.

INGREDIENTS

- 3 tbsp unsalted butter
- 1 large shallot, diced
- 8 oz (230 g) cream cheese, softened
- 1 cup (250 mL) sour cream
- 1 cup (250 mL) half and half
- 1 ½ cups (375 mL) shredded sharp white cheddar cheese
- ¼ cup (60 mL) freshly squeezed lemon juice
- 2 tbsp Worcestershire sauce
- 1 tsp ground cayenne pepper
- 1 tbsp Old Bay seasoning
- 1 tbsp dry mustard
- 1 tsp salt
- ½ tsp freshly ground black pepper
- 1 (500 g) lb lump crabmeat, picked over for shells, rinsed, and drained
- 8 oz (230 g) canned mild green chiles, drained
- 2 tbsp unsalted butter (for breadcrumbs)
- ¾ cup (175 mL) fresh white breadcrumbs
- 1 tsp smoked paprika
- 3 tbsp chopped fresh parsley, for garnish

IF YOU'D LIKE TO ADD SPICE TO THIS RECIPE, THROW A DICED JALAPEÑO PEPPER IN WITH THE SHALLOTS AS THEY SAUTÉ.

TAPENADE TRIO

These simple recipes were created by Heidi to serve at studio and gallery openings in the Northeast Minneapolis Arts District. With so many starving-artist friends in our neighborhood, we found a need for affordable, flavorful appetizers. Serve with fresh pita bread or pita chips.

ARTICHOKE TAPENADE

In a food processor, combine artichokes, cheese, lemon juice, garlic, and salt. Process until well combined. Turn off processor and scrape down sides. With processor on, slowly add olive oil and continue to process until smooth. Transfer to serving bowl and stir in parsley. Garnish with whole parsley leaves.

Makes about 1 cup (250 mL). (GF) (V)

KALAMATA TAPENADE

In a food processor, purée olives and capers with lemon juice. Drizzle in olive oil, 1 tbsp at a time, until consistency is smooth. Stir well and continue to purée, adding thyme, salt, and pepper.

With a spatula, transfer tapenade to serving bowl. Garnish with whole sprigs of fresh thyme.

Makes about 1 cup (250 mL). (DF) (GF) (VV)

RED PEPPER TAPENADE

In a small frying pan, toast almonds on medium heat for 2–3 minutes until lightly browned. (Do not get distracted by a phone call! It only takes a matter of seconds to burn an entire batch of nuts.) Transfer to a food processor, add remainder of ingredients, and process until smooth.

Makes about 1 cup (250 mL). (DF) (GF) (VV)

TIP: ALL THREE TAPENADES CAN BE MADE
SEVERAL DAYS IN ADVANCE.

INGREDIENTS

Artichoke Tapenade

1 cup (250 mL) canned artichoke hearts, drained
¼ cup (60 mL) grated Parmesan cheese
1 tbsp freshly squeezed lemon juice
1 garlic clove, coarsely chopped
½ tsp salt
3 tbsp olive oil
1 tbsp finely chopped Italian parsley
whole parsley leaves, for garnish

Kalamata Tapenade

1 cup (250 mL) pitted Kalamata olives, drained and rinsed
1 tbsp capers, drained and rinsed
2 tbsp freshly squeezed lemon juice
¼ cup (60 mL) olive oil
2 sprigs fresh thyme leaves, coarsely chopped, plus more for garnish
½ tsp kosher salt
½ tsp freshly ground black pepper

Red Pepper Tapenade

¼ cup (60 mL) slivered almonds
1 cup (250 mL) canned red peppers, drained
2 garlic cloves, chopped
½ tsp salt
¼ cup (60 mL) olive oil

CHOWGIRLS TAPENADE TRIO IS EASY TO MAKE AND OFFERS SOMETHING FOR EVERYONE.

THE DRIZZLE OF BROWN BUTTER AT THE FINISH TAKES THIS SIMPLE SIPPER OVER THE TOP.

BECCA'S BUTTERNUT BISQUE

A colorful respite in the cold winter months, this recipe was perfected by Becca, who's worn multiple chef hats at Chowgirls. The velvety texture and expertly balanced flavors of this seasonal soup shot are a testament to her talent!

Preheat oven to 350°F (180°C) and line a baking sheet with parchment paper.

In a large bowl, drizzle squash pieces with olive oil and toss to coat

Spread squash pieces in a single layer on parchment-lined baking sheet and roast, turning once, for 1 hour or until pieces are softened and browned at the edges.

Meanwhile, in a medium stock pot on medium heat, melt butter. Add onions and sauté on low heat for 10 minutes, until they have sweated down and moisture has evaporated from pan. Increase heat to medium-high, stir onions frequently and scrape up caramelization from bottom of pan. Once onions are medium-brown, add garlic and sauté for 2 minutes, stirring frequently. Increase heat to high and deglaze pan with white wine and champagne vinegar. Continue to cook for about 5 minutes to reduce liquids.

After wine and vinegar have almost completely evaporated from pan, add roasted squash, broth, salt, and cream. Cook on medium-low heat for 10–15 minutes or until squash starts to break down. Transfer soup to a blender and blend on high until soup appears creamy and smooth. (Be careful when blending hot liquids!) Pass soup mixture through strainer. Add sherry vinegar and salt to taste.

In a small saucepan on medium heat, melt 3 tbsp butter and cook for 1–2 minutes, until solids start to brown. Keep warm.

Pour soup into shot glasses. Top each with ½ tsp brown butter and ¼ tsp pistachios.

Makes 18 to 24 shots.

INGREDIENTS

- 2 lb (900 g) butternut squash, peeled and cubed
- 1 tbsp olive oil
- 5 tbsp (75 mL) butter
- 2 ½ cups (625 mL) chopped yellow onions
- 4 garlic cloves, peeled and minced
- ½ cup (125 mL) white wine
- 2 tbsp champagne vinegar
- 4 cups (1 L) vegetable broth
- 3 tbsp kosher salt
- ¾ cup (175 mL) heavy cream
- 2 tbsp sherry vinegar
- salt, to taste
- 3 tbsp salted butter
- 3 tbsp pistachios, chopped, for garnish

(GF) (V)

CORN PANCAKES WITH CARNITAS & PICKLED RED ONION

A guaranteed crowd pleaser. You can make the pickled onions and carnitas a day ahead for this Chowgirls favorite, then prepare the pancakes when you're ready to serve them. This goes great with our Guacamole and Pico de Gallo recipes (p. 52) and, of course, a cold margarita!

GARNISH

In a small bowl, combine sliced onions and vinegar. Cover and chill for at least 6 hours. (Can be stored in a refrigerator for up to 2 weeks—and they get better with age.)

PORK

Preheat oven to 375°F (190°C).

Trim pork shoulder of excess fat and rub with olive oil, garlic, 3 tsp salt, pepper, cumin, and thyme. Place pork in a heavy Dutch oven and sear on high heat, 3–4 minutes each side, until browned. Add orange quarters and orange juice. Add 1 cup (250 mL) water. Cover pot and bake, turning occasionally, for 1 ½ hours. Remove lid and cook for 30 more minutes or until meat is tender and easily torn. Discard oranges. Cool pork slightly and pull into long strips. Lightly chop pork, place in a bowl, and pour pan drippings over it. Taste and season with salt and pepper. Keep warm.

CORN CAKES

In a medium bowl, whisk together cornmeal, flour, ½ tsp salt, and baking powder. Add egg, honey, milk, and melted butter, and whisk to combine. Lightly oil a griddle or large frying pan on high heat until almost smoking. Reduce heat to medium and, using a tablespoon measure, pour small pancake rounds. Cook about 1 minute, turn, and cook second side until browned. Remove from heat and keep warm.

Top each pancake with crème fraîche and pulled pork. Garnish with pickled onions and cilantro.

Makes about 24 adorable little snacks.

INGREDIENTS

Garnish
½ small red onion, center removed, thinly sliced
¼ cup (60 mL) red wine vinegar

Pork
2 lb (900 g) boneless pork shoulder
2 tbsp olive oil
3 garlic cloves, minced
3 tsp salt
1 tsp freshly ground black pepper
1 tsp ground cumin
2 tsp chopped fresh thyme
1 orange, quartered
1 cup (250 mL) orange juice

Corncakes
¾ cup (175 mL) cornmeal
¼ cup (60 mL) all-purpose flour
½ tsp salt
1 tsp baking powder
1 egg, beaten
1 tbsp honey
1 cup (250 mL) milk
1 tbsp butter, melted
1 cup crème fraîche
¼ cup (60 mL) chopped cilantro, for garnish

ANYONE WHO LIKES TACOS IS GOING TO FLIP OVER THESE CORN CAKES!

TRADITIONALLY, PASTIES ARE FILLED WITH RUTABAGA AND TURNIPS. WE UPDATED THE ROOT VEGGIES WITH SUNCHOKES AND PARSNIPS. FEEL FREE TO SUBSTITUTE WITH THE FORMER.

IRON RANGE PASTIES

Not to be confused with the pastie (pronounced PAY-stee) featured in burlesque shows, the pasty (pronounced PASS-tee) is a pocket pastry popular in areas along Lake Superior, particularly the Upper Peninsula of Michigan and the Iron Range of Minnesota. This recipe is one of Heidi's originals, inspired by her Midwest roots and favorite root veggies.

Preheat oven to 350°F (180°C).

In a large pot on high heat, blanch sunchokes, parsnips, carrots, and potatoes in boiling water for 3 minutes. Set aside to cool. Mix dry spices into ground pork. Add vegetables. Arrange pie crust rounds on a baking sheet. Place 1½ tbsp meat mixture onto half of each round. With your fingertip, brush water along edge of pie crusts. Fold crust over mixture, and crimp shut with fork tines. Bake for 15–20 minutes, until lightly browned.

Makes 24 pasties, 32 if you're a high roller!

INGREDIENTS

½ cup (125 mL) peeled and diced
    sunchokes, ¼-in (6-mm) pieces
½ cup (125 mL) peeled and diced parsnips,
    ¼-in (6-mm) pieces
¾ cup (175 mL) peeled and diced carrots,
    ¼-in (6-mm) pieces
¾ cup (175 mL) peeled and diced
    potatoes, ¼-in (6-mm) pieces
1 tsp freshly ground black pepper
1 tsp anise seeds
1 tsp ground paprika
1 tsp ground fennel seeds
1 tsp whole fennel seeds
1 tsp onion flakes
1 tsp garlic powder
½ tsp red pepper flakes
2 tsp salt
1 lb (500 g) ground beef or pork
2 9-in (23-cm) pie crusts (recipe, p. 62),
    rolled and cut into 2.5-in (6.35-cm)
    rounds

TO BE THE HOST WITH THE MOST
FOR YOUR VEGETARIAN FRIENDS, OMIT
THE MEAT AND DOUBLE THE ROOT
VEGETABLE QUANTITIES.

(V)

WINTER SQUASH & SAUSAGE SKEWERS

Butternut squash is our favorite cold-storage vegetable. The addition of browned butter, fried sage leaves, and sweet maple syrup to savory, salty Italian sausage and caramelized squash takes this winter kebab to a whole new level. In-house we lovingly call these "squasages," a tongue twister that never gets old, no matter that we serve them almost daily during the cold seasons.

Preheat oven to 350° (180°C).

In a large bowl, toss together cubed squash, 1 tbsp olive oil, salt, and pepper. Arrange in a single layer on a parchment-lined baking sheet. Bake for 30 minutes. Toss and cook another 25 minutes, until lightly browned. On a second baking sheet, place sausage links and baste with 1 tbsp olive oil. Bake for 25 minutes. Set squash and sausages aside and let cool slightly.

On a cutting board, cut each sausage link into 1-in (2.5-cm) chunks. Skewer pieces of sausage and squash on 5-in (12-cm) bamboo or metal skewers and arrange in a single layer on a clean platter.

In a small frying pan on medium-high heat, melt butter. Add sage leaves and cook about 30–40 seconds, until butter starts to brown and sage leaves begin to sizzle. This should take less than a minute, so watch carefully or the butter will burn. Quickly stir in maple syrup and immediately remove from heat. Drizzle over squash and sausage skewers. Serve warm.

Makes about 30 skewers.

INGREDIENTS

1 butternut squash (about 2 ½ lb [1 kg]), peeled and cut into 1-in (2.5-cm) cubes
1 tbsp olive oil
1 tsp kosher salt
freshly ground black pepper to taste
5 mild Italian sausage links
1 tbsp olive oil
¼ cup (60 mL) unsalted butter, sliced thinly
3 tbsp torn sage leaves
3 tbsp real maple syrup

CUTTING THE SAUSAGE AFTER IT'S COOKED ENSURES THAT IT WILL BE SUCCULENT AND NOT DRY.

LOCAL BEER FONDUE

Our kitchen and headquarters are in Northeast Minneapolis, an area famous for eclectic art, re-purposed warehouse space, and craft beer taprooms. We love pairing local beers with our food and, in this case, cooking with it! Serve with cubed baguette and raw vegetables.

In a small bowl, toss cheddar and semi-soft cheese chunks with flour and cornstarch until well coated. Set aside.

Into a medium saucepan, add beer and stir in nutmeg, mustard, and lemon juice. Warm on medium heat until just bubbling, then add flour-dredged cheeses, whisking continuously until melted, about 5 minutes.

Rub peeled garlic clove along inside of fondue bowl, then pour in melted cheese mixture. Keep warm in a fondue pot, stirring occasionally and ensuring that the bottom does not burn.

Makes 2 cups (500 mL).

INGREDIENTS

- ½ lb (250 g) sharp cheddar cheese (preferably local), shredded
- ½ lb (250 g) semi-soft cheese (similar to Camembert; preferably local), cut into chunks
- 1 tbsp all-purpose flour
- 1 tbsp cornstarch
- 1 cup (250 mL) local beer (Pilsner-style is best)
- ⅛ tsp freshly ground nutmeg
- 2 tsp dry mustard
- 1 tsp lemon juice
- 1 garlic clove, peeled

CRaFT BREWERiES aRE POPPiNG UP LiKE DaNDELiONS EVERYWHERE! YOU COULD TRY THiS RECiPE WiTH a DiFFERENT LOCaL BEER EVERY WEEK UNTiL YOU'VE FOUND YOUR FaVORiTE COMBiNaTiON.

BEETS & BURRATA

This vegetarian small plate pairs dressed roasted beets with burrata cheese—a creamy hybrid of mozzarella and ricotta that's a current rage among foodies. Topping it with toasted macadamia nuts and a spray of microgreens adds crunch and color.

Preheat oven to 400°F (200°C).

If using small beets, quarter them. If beets are large, cut them into 1 ½-in (4-cm) wedges. In a large bowl, toss beets with 2 tbsp olive oil, salt, and pepper to coat well. Spread on a parchment-lined baking sheet in a single layer and bake, turning once, for about 40 minutes or until cooked through and slightly crispy. Remove from oven and let cool.

While cooling beets, make dressing. In a small bowl, blend vinegar, orange zest, and juice. Slowly add ¼ cup olive oil, whisking continuously, until mixture thickens. Season with salt and pepper. Pour dressing over cooled beets and toss well.

On a clean cutting board, slice each ball of burrata into quarters. To assemble dish, place a piece of burrata on each plate, tuck in 2–3 beets, and top with macadamia nuts and microgreens. Serve cold or at room temperature.

Makes 16 to 24 small plates.

INGREDIENTS

4–6 beets, tops removed, peeled
2 tbsp olive oil
2 tsp kosher salt
1 tsp fresh ground black pepper
2 tbsp red wine vinegar
zest of 1 orange
juice of 1 orange
¼ cup (60 mL) olive oil
salt and pepper to taste
1 lb (500 g) burrata, drained
½ cup (125 mL) chopped toasted
  macadamia nuts
1 cup (250 mL) fresh microgreens or
  watercress

YOUR LiFE WiLL BE a LOT EASiER iF YOU ZEST THE ORANGE BEFORE JUiCiNG iT.

WE LOVE TO USE A MIXTURE OF RED AND GOLDEN BEETS FOR VISUAL INTEREST.

WE LIKE THE CLEAN TASTE OF
BEELER'S PORK FROM THE
LOESS HILLS OF WESTERN IOWA
WHERE FREE-ROAMING PIGS
ARE RAISED WITH CARE AND
RESPECT.

PORK TENDERLOIN WITH CHERRY-ROSEMARY MARMALADE

One of our most original and perennially popular combinations, this pork and cherry pairing looks great as a small plate—or sliced on a wooden carving board with the marmalade on the side, garnished with fresh rosemary sprigs.

PORK

Heat a gas or charcoal grill to about 375°F (190°C). If using a broiler, preheat to 525°F (275°C) and preheat a baking sheet or broiler pan.

Rinse pork tenderloin and pat dry. In a small bowl, stir together salt, pepper, parsley, and garlic. Rub spice mixture on pork tenderloin, covering it completely, and set aside.

When grill is ready, place tenderloin in the center and close lid. Roast for 12–15 minutes, turning about every 3 minutes, until tenderloin is nicely browned and reaches an internal temperature of 160° F (70°C). If broiling, place tenderloin on preheated baking sheet, 3–4 in (8–10 cm) from flame, and roast for 10 minutes per side.

Allow pork to rest for 10 minutes, then carve and serve with Cherry-Rosemary Marmalade.

Makes 8–12 appetizer servings, depending on how ravenous your guests are.

MARMALADE

In a large frying pan on medium, heat olive oil until sizzling, then add shallots and garlic. Sauté for 2–3 minutes, until slightly softened. Increase heat to high and add wine, stirring well, until reduced by half. Stir in cherries and broth, reduce heat to medium-low, and cook, stirring occasionally, for 15 minutes or until cherries have softened and mixture takes on a glossy appearance. Stir in chopped rosemary, salt, and pepper. Let cool slightly before serving. Can be refrigerated for up to 2 weeks.

Makes 1 cup (250 mL).

INGREDIENTS

Pork

1 pork tenderloin (about
   2 lb/900 g)
1 ½ tsp kosher salt
1 tsp freshly ground black pepper
¼ cup (60 mL) finely chopped fresh
   parsley
2 garlic cloves, minced

Marmalade

2 tbsp olive oil
3 small shallots, diced
2 garlic cloves, minced
½ cup (125 mL) white wine
1 cup (250 mL) dried cherries, coarsely
   chopped
1 cup (250 mL) chicken or vegetable broth
2 tsp finely chopped fresh rosemary
salt and pepper, to taste

LEFTOVER CHERRY-ROSEMARY MARMALADE IS A GREAT ADDITION TO ANY CHEESE PLATE, TOO. WE ESPECIALLY LIKE IT WITH TRIPLE-CREAM BRIE!

DF GF

DUCK À L'ORANGE FIRECRACKER ROLLS

Lucky enough to live in a neighborhood packed with Asian markets and delis, Amy fell in love with the rich and mysterious flavor of Chinese roast duck and has developed a handful of recipes that incorporate it. These were originally made for a friend's French-themed, appetizer-heavy wedding. Serve hot with sweet and sour sauce for dipping.

In a large stock pot, bring 2 qt (2 L) salted water to a boil. Blanch cabbage for 1–2 minutes until wilted. Strain and cool slightly. Wrap cabbage in a clean dish towel and wring out excess water. Place cabbage in a medium bowl. Add ginger, garlic, orange zest, duck, sesame oil, oyster sauce, salt, and white pepper, and stir to combine.

To make rolls, lay a wonton wrapper on a cutting board in a diamond position. Place about 1 tsp filling in center. Fold in sides so that corners touch filling.

Starting from the bottom, roll wrapper up to cover filling, tucking it in as you roll. Using your fingertip, dab a bit of water on top corner, then fold it over to seal roll. Lay prepped rolls on wax or parchment paper dusted with cornstarch to prevent sticking.

In a large frying pan on high, heat oil until almost smoking. Reduce heat to medium-high and add eggrolls in batches, being careful not to overcrowd pan. Cook for about 2 minutes each side, remove with tongs, and transfer to a paper towel-lined plate until ready to serve.

Makes about 30 rolls.

INGREDIENTS

1 tsp salt (for blanching cabbage)
1 lb (500 g) napa cabbage, thinly sliced
1 tbsp peeled and chopped fresh ginger
3 garlic cloves, chopped
2 tsp orange zest
½ lb (250 g) roasted Chinese duck meat, chopped
1 tsp toasted sesame oil
2 tsp oyster sauce
½ tsp kosher salt (for filling)
¼ tsp white pepper
1 package square wheat-based wonton wrappers
cornstarch, for dusting parchment
¾ cup (175 mL) sunflower, peanut, or other light oil

CHOWGIRLS GLÖGG

There's an undeniable Scandinavian presence in Minnesota; it's in the names (every other person is an Anderson or an Olson), the fashion, the seasons, and the cuisine. We like this mulled Nordic drink because it's especially comforting on gray snowy days. And it has an umlaut in its name. More umlauts for everyone!

In a large pot, mix together all ingredients. Warm on medium heat; be careful not to boil. Reduce heat to medium-low and simmer for 45 minutes. Strain into a slow cooker to keep it warm throughout the party. Use a ladle to pour into mugs. Serve warm.

Makes 12 cups (3 L).

INGREDIENTS

2 26-oz (750 mL) bottles red wine
4 cups (1 L) brandy
10 cardamom pods, cracked
5 star anise
5 whole cloves
3 cinnamon sticks
1 cup (250 mL) sugar
1 cup (250 mL) sliced or slivered almonds
1 cup (250 mL) pitted dates

TRADITIONALLY THIS RECIPE WOULD CALL FOR RAISINS OR PRUNES. WE LIKE THE MORE EXOTIC FLAVOR OF DATES. FEEL FREE TO SUBSTITUTE IF YOU PREFER OTHERWISE.

SAGE WOODSTOCK

The bright juice of Meyer lemons contrasts nicely with the woodsy tones of maple syrup and botanical fragrances of juniper and sage, like the sun bursting through the stark branches of a maple tree in the bright white snow. A crisp sip with a smooth finish, this is the cocktail that converted Heidi into a gin drinker.

In a medium pot on high heat, bring water to a boil. Add sage leaves and maintain a rolling boil for 10–15 minutes, until liquid is reduced by half. Remove from heat and strain out sage leaves. Immediately stir maple syrup into liquid until completely combined. Set aside to cool.

Meanwhile, use a paring knife to slice thin oval pieces of lemon peel, about the size of a bottle cap. Set aside in a small bowl for garnish. Cut lemons in half and extract juice. Strain pulp and pour 3 cups (700 mL) lemon juice into blender. When syrup is cool, add to lemon juice and blend to create a mixer. Just before serving, shake equal amounts mixer and gin over ice. Strain and pour into martini glasses. Twist lemon peel over each cocktail to extract essential oil, then drop in to float in drinks.

Makes 8 cocktails.

INGREDIENTS

3 cups (700 mL) water
10 whole leaves fresh sage
1 ½ cups (375 mL) maple syrup
9 Meyer lemons
1 26-oz (750-mL) bottle gin

JUST AS THE CRAFT BREWERY BOOM PEAKED, OUR NEIGHBORHOOD WAS CLAIMED AS TURF BY ANOTHER LIQUID VICE PUSHER—THE LOCAL DISTILLERY. CONSIDER THIS A GREAT EXCUSE TO TRY A GIN THAT'S MADE CLOSE TO HOME.

THE WOODSTOCK IS A WONDERFUL WAY TO SHINE THE SPOTLIGHT ON THE UNIQUE FLAVOR OF THE MEYER LEMON.

HOT ROD TODDY

Fueled with bourbon and spice, this little red Corvette of warm boozy flavors pays homage to Heidi's Motor City heritage. Local honey and a clove-studded orange sweeten the ride.

In a large pot on high heat, bring water to a boil. Add whole spices and simmer for 10 minutes. Remove from heat, add loose black tea, and steep for 10 minutes. Strain tea into thermal container. Stir in honey until dissolved. Keep hot until ready to serve.

Cut orange in half lengthwise and then each half lengthwise again into quarters. Pierce peel of each wedge with tip of paring knife, three times, equally spaced. Push whole cloves into piercings.

To mix each drink, pour 2 oz (60 mL) bourbon into ceramic or tempered glass mug, top with 6 oz (180 mL) tea mixture, and stir. Garnish with a clove-studded orange wedge and cinnamon stick.

Makes 8 toddies.

INGREDIENTS

8 cups (2 L) water
3 cinnamon sticks
6 whole cloves
6 pink peppercorns
6 cardamom pods
3 star anise
1 cup (250 mL) loose black tea
½ cup (125 mL) honey (preferably local)
1 orange, for garnish
24 whole cloves, for garnish
2 cups (500 mL) bourbon
8 cinnamon sticks, for garnish

AS THE DAY GOES ON, YOU MAY WISH TO INCREASE THE RATIO OF BOURBON TO TEA. FOLLOW YOUR INSTINCT. IT'LL BE OUR LITTLE SECRET.

POP'S EGGNOG

Amy's mother-in-law recently shared this wonderful from-scratch eggnog recipe that was created by her father, the beloved "Pop" Manning. It's boozy, frothy, and delicious—consider this your new "master recipe" for eggnog season. Pop used Four Roses Bourbon.

In a stand mixer, combine egg whites with half the sugar and beat until stiff. Combine remainder of sugar with egg yolks in a separate bowl and stir well.

Add yolks to egg-white mixture and beat until blended. Stir in cream, milk, bourbon, and rum. Serve very cold.

Makes 8 cups (2 L).

INGREDIENTS

6 eggs, separated
¾ cup (175 mL) sugar
2 cups (500 mL) heavy cream
2 cups (500 mL) milk
2 cups (500 mL) bourbon whiskey
2 oz (60 mL) dark Jamaican rum

SINCE AMY HAILS FROM KENTUCKY, WE'LL ALWAYS BE PARTIAL TO BOURBON WHISKEY. FEEL FREE TO SUBSTITUTE YOUR FAVORITE, WHETHER IT'S FROM TENNESSEE, CANADA, OR EUROPE. YOUR HOUSE—YOU CALL, AND DRINK, THE SHOTS.

ACKNOWLEDGMENTS

Thanks to everyone who's helped us realize our vision for this cookbook and more.

Publishing pals: Our brilliant agent Michael Croy of Northstar Literary Agency; Brian Lam, Robert Ballantyne, Susan Safyan, and Cynara Geissler, of Arsenal Pulp Press; Steve Horowitz; Consortium's Julie Schaper and Bill Mockler; and all of Amy's other book club friends.

Production slingers: LoAnn Mockler and Carolyn Jensen for gunning through the proofing process.

Creative advisors: Robert Pflaum, Chank Diesel, Jeff Johnson, and Lucas Richards.

Photography: Jennifer Marx, Shelly Mosman, and Sarah Whiting, whose posse of college students have kept us in good photographic standing for many moons.

Recipe testers: LoAnn Mockler, Lisa Turnham, Suzanne Marx, Kate O'Reilly, Steve Cohen, Alex Freese, Joe Berens, Sue Meger, Chank Diesel, Krystal Gee Follis, and Meghan McAndrews.

Chowgirls staff, past and present: Big thanks to y'all for helping us stay inspired, in business, and loved. A special shout-out to Ari, Becca, Maari, Onno, Meg, Maren, and Jenny for sharing your recipes with us!

Business mentors: Todd Churchill, founder of Thousand Hills Cattle Co.; Ari Weinzweig, Zingerman's Community of Businesses; Kieran Folliard, 2 Gingers Irish Whiskey and The Food Building; Alex Roberts, Brasa and Alma; Patisserie 46's John Kraus; Nancy Lyons, Clockwork; Robert Stephens, founder of Geek Squad; Bill Kling, founder of Minnesota Public Radio; Nancy Hovanes of Oak Creek Partners; Davis Senseman of Davis Law, and Heidi's hero, Foo Fighter Dave Grohl.

Amy's friends & family: My parents, Dan and Lynn Brown, for being great home cooks; my husband, Eric Levy, for being patient while I grew a company; my oldest friend, Su Jang, caterer extraordinaire, for teaching me how to cook Chinese food back in the old days; the Kirchoff's Bakery family in Paducah, Kentucky; and my "sister-wife" and Chowgirls' sales director, Maari Cedar-James, for being a joy to cook and work with.

Heidi's friends & family: My clean-plate-club husband Chank and super-taster son Max; my parents, Maxine & Jim Murray and Randy Olmack & Beverly Thoel, for letting me do my own thing; my late grandmothers, Ila Olmack, for passing on the catering genes, and Martha Molotky, for teaching me our Polish family recipes; my high school friends' parents Ralph Schillace and Catherine LaRose for sharing their Sicilian passion for cooking and eating; and the Uppercut crew—Lisa, Alex, Heidi, Joe, Ray, Alfonso, and Seko—for being such good eaters.

INDEX

Note: Photographs denoted by page numbers in *italics*.